PRAYER AND FASTING

THE MYSTERIES UNLOCKED

PERCY R. WELSING

Prayer and Fasting the Mysteries Unlocked

The author was motivated to write this book by life experiences. Within its pages, he has included several individual and personal testimonies as a means of encouraging others to draw closer to the Lord through prayer and fasting. He uses the Bible as a key to unlock the mystery of prayer and fasting.

In this book many questions have been answered on the topic of prayer and fasting in very plain and simple language, and have addressed issues regarding our relationship with God. This book will equip the reader with knowledge and understanding of prayer and fasting in addition to what you already know. The explanatory approach on the subject will help the reader apply the principles of prayer and fasting that will serve to develop a personal relationship with God.

The author holds bachelors degrees in Science and Religious Education and a Masters degree in Science Education. He applies his knowledge in these disciplines to explain spiritual truths and he makes scripture read like a novel.

Words of Commendation

Prayer and Fasting The Mysteries Unlocked by Brother Percy R. Welsing was an excellent resource and teaching tool for me when I taught a three-part series on fasting to my congregation. To any Pastor who is endeavoring to take his congregation to another level of understanding regarding prayer and fasting, this book is a must.

Pastor Luke A. McClendon
Christ Temple Apostolic Church
Westland, Michigan

If you have ever been unsure or had questions about prayer and fasting, look no further. *Prayer and Fasting, The Mysteries Unlocked* will give the clarity that every believer needs when it comes to communicating with God and bringing their flesh under subjection through fasting. It is not a complicated or convoluted book with a lot of hard to understand ideas, but to the contrary, it is easy to read and comprehend. Reading this book has enlightened me even more in these areas and I believe everyone who reads this book will gain valuable insight and will be blessed.

First Lady Crisette Ellis
Greater Grace Temple
Detroit, Michigan

This is an insightful, Bible-based book on prayer and fasting. Percy's book is easy to follow and destined to impact the reader's prayer life. This is a must read for every Christian. It will change the way you look at prayer and the seriousness with which you approach fasting.

Dr. & Mrs. Charles Appeadu
Atlanta, Georgia

Reading this book has brought about an enlightenment to my understanding of victories we can receive when we adhere to the Word of God. Percy and Gloria Welsing have been used mightily through revelation from God. This book will empower, strengthen, encourage and direct you to a higher level of thinking and living in Christ Jesus.

LaShawn Stevenson
Detroit, Michigan

This is the most awesome book I have ever read on prayer and fasting. It has blessed me tremendously. You cannot put this book down when you start reading it! It will help you get to the place in Matthew 17:21 where it says, "...this kind goeth not out but by prayer and fasting." The Lord has truly blessed Percy and Gloria Welsing in the writing of this book.

Rev. Delores (Pat) Britt
Kadesh Baptist Church
Plymouth, Michigan

Prayer and Fasting
the Mysteries Unlocked

Copyright © 2004, 2008 by Percy R. Welsing

P.O. Box 401316
Redford, MI 48240
E-mail: pwelsing@sbcglobal.net
Available on www.amazon.com

Series Publishing
Toll Free: 1-866-543-9184

Library of Congress 2004, 2008
ISBN 0-9723328-0-4

Printed in the United States of America

Dedication

*Dedicated to Gloria, my wife and Co-Author,
for her love, support and hard work.*

*To my late mother, Mercy, for her hard work, selfless-
ness and motherly love through the years. May her
soul rest in peace.*

*To all prayer warriors around the world and those
who wish to come closer to God through prayer and
fasting.*

Table of Contents

PART FOUR
Dynamics of Prayer

PART FIVE
Types of Prayer

PART SIX
Principles of Prayer

PART SEVEN
Prayer is the Key

PART EIGHT
Why Should We Fast?

PART NINE
Recipients of a Blessing

Acknowledgements

I thank the Almighty God the only sovereign judge who has counted us worthy to write this book.

I appreciate Bishop Charles H. Ellis III, Senior Pastor of Greater Grace Temple and Rev. Dr. Jessica Kendall Ingram, Episcopal Supervisor of African Methodist Episcopal Church for writing the forwards to this book.

I am thankful to Trustee Martin Hardy of Greater Grace Temple for reading through the manuscript.

My regards to Rev. Dr. Louis Tuffour, Chaplain of Providence Hospital for his role in editing the manuscript.

Sister Fran Carter of Greater Grace and Pat Hicks of Family Christian Bookstores took pains to edit the manuscript, for which I am very grateful.

My appreciation goes to Ms. Ann-Marie Richardson who was willing and dedicated to the typing of the manuscript and Mrs. E'Shaun Caine for her diligence and commitment to the typesetting which has made this vision a reality. I am also thankful to Dr. Samuel Koranteng-Pipim, Director of Public Campus Ministries for the Michigan Conference, Author and an Adjunct Professor who assisted with the publication procedures.

God richly bless you all, and other friends and brethren who have contributed in diverse ways to the success of this book.

Foreword I

In this book, Percy Welsing endeavors to reveal many important truths regarding our spiritual relationship with Christ Jesus. The Bible emphatically declares to us that much of our overcoming of the various snares, pitfalls and temptations of the devil is dependent on our consistency in prayer and fasting. Percy shares many examples of how prayer and fasting contributes to being a productive Christian who is walking in victory. And you too, can declare yourself a successful overcomer.

I am certain that you will be inspired, uplifted, encouraged and informed as you meditate in this powerful teaching on prayer and fasting. I further believe that these truths within will challenge you to be more committed to the awesome spiritual weapons of prayer and fasting. Remember St. Paul's words in Ephesians 6:12, "For we wrestle not against flesh and blood, but against principalities, against powers, against the rulers of the darkness of this world, against spiritual wickedness in high places." Paul cautions us to meet spiritual attacks with spiritual weapons.

In closing, let me admonish you to begin to practice what you read in this book and watch God bring you many immediate results. After all, it is our tests and trials that present opportunities for God to demonstrate His power and awesomeness. And the way to access this power is through prayer and fasting. Remember the words of Jesus in Matthew 17:21, "…this kind goeth not out but by prayer and fasting." Be blessed.

Bishop Charles H. Ellis III
Senior Pastor, Greater Grace Temple
Assistant Presiding Bishop, PAW, Inc.

Foreword II

I have been a student of the spiritual disciplines of prayer and fasting for more than twenty-five years. Because of my passion for the spiritual growth of others as well as for myself, I have been intentional about reading the works of those persons who have expertise in this area.

My library includes many books by some of the most noted authorities on the spiritual disciplines from the desert Fathers such as Father Lawrence to contemporary writers such as Brennan Manning. And while I must say that I have been tremendously blessed and I have matured in my understanding of prayer and fasting through these inspired materials, none of them have been as inspirational and as thorough as the work of these authors.

I was pleasantly surprised and impressed with the comprehensive nature of Prayer and Fasting, The Mysteries Unlocked. The authors have supplied us with an in-depth biblically based understanding of prayer and fasting.

It is obvious that the authors did not write this work based upon theory or what they have heard from others. I sense and know that this much needed book is based upon their personal experience with God and having learned first hand the power of prayer and fasting in their lives. The book has an appeal both to the novice and to the seasoned person who has been practicing the spiritual disciplines.

Get ready to be tremendously blessed. Get ready for a significant spiritual change to take place in your life. And because this book will catapult you to another level in God, be sure to purchase one for a friend and many for persons in your church. Watch the joy that comes into their lives as the mysteries are unlocked.

Rev. Dr. Jessica Kendall Ingram
Episcopal Supervisor
African Methodist Episcopal Church

Preface

This book has come about through revelation by the Holy Spirit about the mystery of prayer and fasting. It all started in a church in South Africa. Living in that part of the world was an experience never to be forgotten. It was during those times that I understood what the Word of God means when it says in James 1:2, "My brethren, count it all joy when ye fall into divers temptations." and in I Thessalonians 5:18 where it is written "In every thing give thanks; for this is the will of God in Christ Jesus concerning you." The fact that the delays of God are not denials became evident to me. This book would never have materialized if I had not gone through persecutions, tests and trials. In fact, "everyone who wants to live a godly life in Christ Jesus will be persecuted" (II Timothy 3:12 NIV).

My wife and I were introduced to a small church community by a friend of ours. It was in that church that we found true fellowship, warmth and enjoyed the sweetness of the presence of God in fellowship. It was there that God opened a new chapter in my understanding of His word.

One blessed day God in His own divine purpose caused the pastor to invite me to take the pulpit on the following Sunday. After that morning, the invitations to preach became more frequent. I call it a divine act of intervention because we were very new in the church and the pastor did not know me. How then could he have entrusted me with the responsibility of steering the spiritual life of his flock. I am thankful to God that most of the messages I preached came as revealed knowledge because I had never heard them before. Hence, I am putting those messages together as the Revelation Series. God said, "And I will give you pastors according to mine heart, which shall feed you with knowledge and understanding" (Jeremiah 3:15). My setbacks have now become set ups for others to be blessed. May God richly bless you as you read these books in this series.

Introduction

Volumes of books have been written on the subject of prayer and fasting and many questions have been answered on these very important subjects. We know that we have to fast and pray because the Bible gives a very clear command that we ought to do so. Our Lord Jesus, the Apostles and many great men of God dead and alive lived lives of prayer and fasting to set an example for us to follow.

I have read books on prayer and fasting by great writers both old and current since the early eighties. They have taught many of us how to pray, where to pray, when to pray, postures in prayer and we may have experienced what happens when the people of God pray. We have also been taught the types of fasting, how to fast, how to break a fast and when to fast. We also know what happens when the people of God fast.

In this book, my main objective is to attempt to answer the question as to what goes on during prayer and fasting that makes them produce results. In other words, my goal is to demystify prayer and fasting in order to make it more understandable and acceptable to the multitude of people who are battling with these subjects. It is my hope that the people of God will see prayer as a privilege and a joy but not a burden in order to be able to build a healthy relationship with our maker. I will also touch on other related issues about these subjects in the course of this book.

It is my hope that as the people of God begin to read this book our faith will increase by receiving answers to our prayers, and we will seize every opportunity we have to fast and pray. I believe this book will equip the people of God with understanding, knowledge and the principles and keys that will translate you into a new world of spiritual and natural breakthroughs.

I hope that this revelation will also give birth to a revival in the lives of many Christians and that a new chapter of spiritual awareness and growth will be opened in their Christian lives. It is very significant that this revelation is revealed especially at a time when the forces of darkness have been unleashed against the body of Christ and on the very creation of God in particular; the September eleven catastrophe and the current spate of wars resulting from religious and cultural differences.

Prayer and fasting are the most powerful spiritual weapons. They are able to reach the unreachable and solve the unsolvable. They have no barriers, unlimited abilities and are more powerful than any physical or spiritual weapon that has ever been manufactured or devised in the history of man. There is no gainsaying that fasting is God's remedy, antidote, a heavenly medication to the sick, solution to man's earthly problems and leads to greater anointing in the ministry.

"For the weapons of our warfare are not carnal, but mighty through God to the pulling down of strong holds; casting down imaginations and every high thing that exalteth itself against the knowledge of God and bringing into captivity every thought to the obedience of Christ" (II Corinthians 10:4, 5).

Rick Warren wrote in Purpose Driven Life, "Prayer is the most important tool for your mission in the world. People may refuse our love or reject our message, but they are defenseless against our prayers. Like an intercontinental missile, you can aim a prayer at a person's heart whether you are ten feet or 10,000 miles away."

Prayer and fasting are the keys that open the door to God's riches of peace, victory, success, healing, deliverance, liberty, spiritual strength and anointing that breaks yokes. The anointing is a result of the divine presence of God that is invoked into our lives during prayer and fasting.

I urge you to read this book from cover to cover. You will be able to complete this book by reading a chapter per day and experience a 42-day evaluation of your prayer and fasting life with the Lord. There is a message that you need to hear. God richly bless you as you read. Please send your comments about your experience to Series Publishing, P.O. Box 401316 Redford, MI 48240.

NOTES:

PART ONE
Phenomenon of Prayer

Chapter 1

The Spiritual Climate

As you stroll the streets of one of the northeastern states of the United States of America, you would be enthused to see a church building almost every three city blocks. In another neighborhood on one street you would be amazed to find a cluster of about ten or more churches next to one another. Furthermore, the national currency is inscribed with these words "In God We Trust." What a blessed land it should be to trust in the Lord because Scripture tells us that "Blessed is the nation whose God is the Lord; and the people whom he hath chosen for his own inheritance" (Psalm 33:12).

We all know too well that spiritual decay is common in our world today and it is interesting to know that around that same neighborhood clustered with churches is the glaring problem of promiscuity, substance abuse and the like. There is a proliferation of churches all right, preaching is going on, but some of the questions to be answered are: "Is our society being impacted by the preaching?" or "Are we enculturating the Christian message?"

Christians are called to be the light of the world and the salt of the earth to preserve society. Hampton Keathly wrote, "We are luminaries in a dark and dismal world." David Yonggi

Cho also said, "In every city, town and community there are church buildings, yet the spirits of worshippers have become empty and void. We have discarded the commandment of the Lord that told us that we should become the light of the world. We have stopped up our ears to the calling of the Holy Spirit."

It is regrettable to say that our light is being dimmed and we have almost lost our saltiness, which is being trodden under the feet of men. It is hard to distinguish between Christians and non-Christians because we are not upholding the standard of the Bible. Scripture says that "Ye shall know them by their fruits" (Matthew 7:16). It is sad to say that the fruits are rare. Church has become more of a routine and lip service rather than seeking to bear the fruits of the Spirit. Scandal has almost become synonymous to the "church." Child molestation, divorce, adultery, fornication, slander, hatred, division, envy, covetousness, lying, wickedness, selfishness, love of money, greediness, pride of life, strife, power struggle and attitudes which do not bring glory to God, have become the order of the day right within the church. Can people look to us and see Christlikeness in us as was seen in the disciples who walked on the streets of Antioch who were distinguished and identified as disciples of Christ? Are we Epistles that could be read by unbelievers?

II Corinthians 3:2,3 says "Ye are our epistle written in our hearts, known and read of all men: Forasmuch as ye are manifestly declared to be the epistle of Christ ministered by us, written not with ink, but with the Spirit of the living God; not in tables of stone, but in fleshy tables of the heart." Our very lives must reflect the image of God if His epistle is written in our hearts. Revelations 3:15,16 says, "I know your deeds that you are neither cold nor hot. I wish you were either one or the other! So, because you are lukewarm- neither hot nor cold- I am about to spit you out of my mouth." God abhors people being lukewarm. We have to be watchful so that our Christian journey will not be in vain because the same God of mercy is also the God of judgment.

I once had an experience in my workplace where I was made to feel very uncomfortable and unwelcome by an individual who was a professing Christian. Almost every other person, including some belonging to other faiths were especially nice to me except the only person who should have been. If I were to describe this person in one word, I would say "mean."

Eddie Gibbs wrote that "Those who have turned to Christianity and churches seeking truth and meaning have left empty-handed, confused by the apparent inability of Christians themselves to implement the principles they profess. Churches, for the most part, have failed to address the nagging anxieties and deep-seated fears of the people, focusing instead upon outdated or secondary issues and proposing tired or trite solutions."

Once on a business trip in South Africa, we did not have enough money to clear our goods from our custom agent. As we negotiated with her, my wife said with all confidence with her shoulders high, "We are Christians, you can clear our goods for us and we will bring the balance later on." Our agent's boss jumped in and responded "Wait a minute, Christians? They lie, they cheat and they kill; the only thing they do is they believe in God." What a sad commentary that was.

If this is true of anyone who has identified with the Lord Jesus, then it is time for repentance, confession and total surrender. It behooves us as Christians to make a difference wherever we find ourselves: on the job, in the school and in the family. We should be a light and salt because the greatest tool of witnessing for the Gospel is our lives.

We could be the only epistle that some people may ever

read. We all have failed together but God is a God of second chances. Because we want to have our way, we have been given over to reprobate minds but God is calling us to come back to Him. II Corinthians 6:17 says, "Wherefore come out from among them, and be ye separate, saith the Lord, and touch not the unclean thing; and I will receive you." Let us open a new chapter, a new direction and like the Apostle Paul, let us press on for the price of the high calling of God. On the day of judgment it is going to be one of two things. God will tell us: "Well done, thou good and faithful servant, enter into your rest" or "I never knew you: depart from me, ye that work iniquity" (Matthew 7:23).

Chapter 2

The Cry of the Soul

We seem to be living in the era of "powerful messages." The devil has tricked us into believing that when we teach and preach about holiness, righteousness, obedience, judgment and hell, people will be discouraged and leave the church. Some preachers have resorted to preaching only messages that will motivate, uplift or bring "encouragement" and "hope" to the congregation. This is good, but we have to preach the Bible in its entirety.

At the end of a church service people say, "Oh! the message was powerful, the message was good" and there it ends, with no application of the message. It is forgotten as we leave the church doors. Satan has almost succeeded in transforming churches into entertainment centers where there is dancing, jumping, clapping and shouting. Many are preaching what the congregation want to hear. At a revival meeting one preacher reiterated what a pastor friend had told him when he was invited to speak at his church. Instead of the pastor praying for God to give the preacher the right message for the congregation, he was told, "Don't be too hard on the people."

We should remember that there is a soul in us that thirsts after God. Messages about holiness, obedience, judgment and hell are those that satisfy, bless, refresh, strengthen and heal the soul. These bring Godly sorrow which lead to repentance. They bring peace and tranquility which no prosperity message can bring. Jesus would not have taught on these subjects if they were out of place. The soul within craves for the things of God but the flesh jumps and claps for the so-called powerful messages which hardly bring any transformation.

Jesus Christ devoted all of the twenty-fourth and twenty-fifth chapters of the gospel of Matthew to teachings on end-times. Let us read what Jesus said in concluding those two chapters. Jesus said in Matthew 25:46 (which is the last verse of the chapter), "And these shall go away into everlasting punishment: but the righteous into life eternal." Even those people who commit crimes have a soul in them that wants to do good. Like Paul, there is something inside of them which wants to do good but they find another member in them that always causes them to do evil (Romans 7:23).

Usually, when messages appeal to the flesh and its desires, we jump, clap and shout, but when messages feed the soul, there is quietness in the church, tears of joy run down the cheeks of people, then comes repentance, salvation, healing, deliverance and transformation. In the third Epistle of John 2 it is written, "I wish above all things that thou mayest prosper and be in health, even as thy soul prospereth." In order for us to be in health and prosper, the soul has to first be prosperous, then we can live in prosperity and in health. Matthew 6:33 says "Seek ye first the kingdom of God, and his righteousness; and all these things shall be added unto you." The soul comes first before the flesh; that is God's "formula" for prosperity, this is God's "equation." If we try to reverse or change the equation, our souls shall starve.

There isn't any number of powerful messages that will satisfy the soul apart from messages on righteousness, holiness, obedience and repentance which appeals to the soul. Let us consider the following verses from the book of Psalms 42:1,2 "As the hart panteth after the water brooks, so panteth my soul after thee, O God. My soul thirsteth for God, for the living God: when shall I come and appear before God?" The soul is longing to be with God, so messages about heaven and hell are those that keep it on track and give encouragement and hope of eternal life to the soul. It is prayer, fasting and the study of the Word of God that humble the soul, and prepares it to meet the Lord.

Rev. Billy Graham is considered the greatest evangelist of our time but for over fifty years of ministry his main verse was John 3:16 which says, "For God so loved the world, that he gave his only begotten Son, that whosoever believeth in him should not perish, but have everlasting life." At his crusades people have wept and given their lives to God because their souls were fed and satisfied. Their souls heard messages that would cause them to appear confidently before their Maker. Proverbs 11:30 says, "...he that winneth souls is wise."

Jesus did not only teach on prosperity. He said, "Labor not for the meat which perisheth, but for that meat which endureth unto everlasting life..." (John 6:27). It is the flesh that is always yearning for material things because the flesh comes from the earth and seeks after the things of the earth. Everything on this earth is from the ground, even our bodies were made from the ground; gold, diamonds, money, buildings, cars, jets, electronic equipment and all that is in this world are from the ground. That is the reason why our flesh is attracted to these things, but the soul thirsts after the righteousness of God. Psalm 63:8a says, "My soul followeth hard after thee."

The soul has a destiny, to appear before God. Hell is not the intended final destination, therefore, our soul cries for God, grieves and yearns after God in order to be with Him. We will be doing our soul a great disservice if we do not work out our salvation with fear and trembling. The last time that I had the privilege of speaking on this subject, people were in tears, repenting and there was diverse reaction to the message. Many responded to the altar call rededicating their lives. Can you believe this? There was more clapping in the church than I had ever experienced in my ministry. I believe that this time the clapping and the celebration were for the deliverance of the soul and it came from the soul and was to the glory of God but not of the flesh.

What we need in the church today is prayer, fasting and the teaching of the unadulterated and balanced Word of God with the urgency that it deserves. I am talking about Biblical fasting and prayer, not "fasting from T.V." and "fasting from shopping" (more on this in Chapter 39).

II Timothy 3:1,2 says in the last days men will be lovers of themselves rather than lovers of God. If men are given the opportunity, we will write our own versions of the Bible because we want to have our way. For example in Mark 10:2-5, Jesus, realizing how the Pharisees wanted to have their way regarding issues of marriage and divorce, said "...For the hardness of your heart he wrote you this precept."

There is so much talk about the fact that things have changed with the passage of time. Reasoning, logic and people's philosophies want to take the place of the Word of God. It is obvious that there are advancements in science and technology but we should be mindful that God had the present generation in mind before He spoke, before He inspired the writers of the Bible, otherwise He could not be omniscient. II Timothy 3:16 says, "All scripture is given by inspiration of God, and is profitable for doctrine, for reproof, for correction, for instruction in righteousness." The Psalmist in 148:6b declares, "he hath made a decree which shall not pass" and the Apostle Paul in his letter to the Romans 8:11 said, "But if the Spirit of him that raised up Jesus from the dead dwell in you, he that raised up Christ from the dead shall also quicken your mortal bodies by his Spirit that dwelleth in you."

The Spirit that inspired the writers of the Bible has decreed that He does not change and His word will not pass away. It is written "Heaven and earth shall pass away, but my words shall not pass away" (Matthew 24:35). This same Spirit which inspired the writers of the gospel and raised Jesus from the dead dwells in us, and has made a decree which shall stand and is still working in us and through us. No matter what the advancements are in science and technology, God and His Word will remain the same.

The Bible talks about the last days when people will be marrying and giving in marriage. Matthew 24:38,39 says, " For as in the days that were before the flood they were eating and drinking, marrying and giving in marriage, until the day that Noe entered into the ark, And knew not until the flood came, and took them all away; so shall also the coming of the Son of man be." These verses have negative connotation because we know that God instituted marriage from the beginning of creation. Genesis 2:18 states; "And the Lord God said, It is not good that the man should be alone; I will make him an help meet for him." Proverbs 18:22 says, "Whoso findeth a wife findeth a good thing, and obtaineth favour of the Lord."

We know that God never contradicts Himself because He is not man that He should forget and He cannot err. God knows that we have to eat and drink to live and He wants us to marry. What displeased God was the same sex marriage and the perversion of the society during Noah's time and what is also happening during our generation. He was displeased with the revellings, drunkenness and ungodliness that existed during

Noah's time and He is saying to us that He is not pleased with the unrighteousness that is almost "engulfing" the church.

As I meditated on this end-time prophecy, I thought of the kind of marriage that is sweeping across the Western world in particular. Homosexuals are being allowed to wed in the church. Some Bishops, Pastors and church leaders are subscribing to and endorsing same sex marriages. The end is nearer than we ever thought. If God endorsed same sex marriages, He would have created Adam and Steve or Adamina and Eve instead of Adam and Eve. If God was not displeased with same sex marriages, then He should not have judged the men and women of Sodom and Gomorrah.

Daniel Migliore wrote, "We are the pinnacle of God's creation," meaning that we are the best thing that God ever made. We were created in the image and likeness of God. God created everything by the word of His mouth, but when He was creating humans He spent time, energy and effort to mold us from the dust of the earth. Though some animal species have been found to exhibit homosexual behavior, the dog happens to be one of the closest to humans in terms of intelligence and sophistication and for that matter the most domesticated of all animals. I have not read, heard or seen two dogs of the same gender such as two male dogs having sex.

The Bible symbolizes dogs as the most base of all creation when it comes to issues of sex and lust. Some humans have brought our standards lower than the dog by having sex with people of the same gender and are even going further to fight for legal rights to marry people of the same sex in the church. What an abomination.

We do not even have to spend time to debate about homosexuality. It is anti-natural law, anti-God, anti-Christ, anti-

Bible, anti-common sense and anti-sanity. Romans 1:26-28 says, "For this cause God gave them up unto vile affections: for even their women did change the natural use into that which is against nature: And likewise also the men, leaving the natural use of the woman, burned in their lust one toward another; men with men working that which is unseemly, and receiving in themselves that recompence of their error which was meet. And even as they did not like to retain God in their knowledge, God gave them over to a reprobate mind, to do those things which are not convenient."

In this contemporary world of postmodernism we are still called not to be of the world. The fact that sin is sin and righteousness is righteousness is a timeless truth and is of universal value. We are changing but God has not changed and His word is still the same. As it is written, "For I am the Lord, I change not;" (Malachi 3:6a).

> **The fact that sin is sin and righteousness is righteousness is a timeless truth and is of universal value.**

In the epistle of Paul to the Galatians 5:19-21 it states, "Now the works of the flesh are manifest, which are these; adultery, fornication, uncleanness, lasciviousness, idolatry, witchcraft, hatred, variance, emulations, wrath, strife, seditions, heresies, envying, murders, drunkenness, revellings, and such like: of the which I tell you before, as I have also told you in time past, that they which do such things shall not inherit the kingdom of God." Even though we are in the world, we are not supposed to be of the world, and therefore, Paul encourages all believers to live by the fruit of the Spirit. He said, "But the fruit of the Spirit is love, joy, peace, long-suffering, gentleness, goodness, faith, meekness, temperance: against such there is no law" (Galatians 5:22,23). In closing, the following is an excerpt to ponder over:

Four Boyfriends

Once upon a time there was this girl who had four boyfriends. She loved the fourth boyfriend the most and adorned him with rich robes and treated him to the finest of delicacies. She gave him nothing but the best.

She also loved the third boyfriend very much and was always showing him off to neighboring kingdoms. However, she feared that one day he would leave her for another.

She also loved her second boyfriend. He was her confidant and was always kind, considerate and patient with her. Whenever this girl faced a problem, she could confide in him, and he would help her get through the difficult times.

The girl's first boyfriend was a very loyal partner and had made great contributions in maintaining her wealth and kingdom. However, she did not love the first boyfriend. Although he loved her deeply, she hardly took notice of him!

One day, the girl fell ill and she knew her time was short. She thought of her luxurious life and wondered, "I now have four boyfriends with me, but when I die, I'll be all alone."

Thus, she asked the fourth boyfriend, "I loved you the most, endowed you with the finest clothing and showered great care over you. Now that I'm dying, will you follow me and keep me company?" "No way!" replied the fourth boyfriend, and he walked away without another word. His answer cut like a sharp knife right into her heart.

The sad girl then asked the third boyfriend, "I loved you all my life. Now that I'm dying, will you follow me and keep me company?" "No!" replied the third boyfriend. "Life is too good! When you die, I'm going to marry someone else!" Her heart sank and turned cold.

She then asked the second boyfriend, "I have always turned to you for help and you've always been there for me. When I die, will you follow me and keep me company?" "I'm sorry, I can't help you out this time!" replied the second boyfriend. "At the very most, I can only walk with you to your grave." His answer struck her like a bolt of lightning, and the girl was devastated.

Then a voice called out, "I'll go with you. I'll follow you no matter where you go." The girl looked up, and there was her first boyfriend. He was very skinny as he suffered from malnutrition and neglect. Greatly grieved, the girl said, "I should have taken much better care of you when I had the chance!"

In truth, you have four boyfriends in your lives:

Your fourth boyfriend is your body. No matter how much time and effort you lavish in making it look good, it will leave you when you die.

Your third boyfriend is your possessions, status and wealth. When you die, it will all go to others.

Your second boyfriend is your family and friends. No matter how much they have been there for you, the furthest they can stay by you is up to the grave.

And your first boyfriend is your Soul, often neglected in pursuit of wealth, power and pleasures of the world.

However, your Soul is the only thing that will follow you

where ever you go. Cultivate, strengthen and cherish it now, for it is the only part of you that will follow you to the throne of God and continue with you throughout Eternity.

This story is an evidence of what Scripture teaches us about the salvation of our souls. The Apostle Paul always tells us over and over again that we should not be ignorant of the devil's devices. It shall not profit us anything if we gain the whole world and lose our souls (Matthew 16:26). We should make the salvation of our souls our priority and work it out with fear and trembling and this truth of the gospel cannot be overemphasized.

Chapter 3

The Missing Link

As I ponder over the spiritual climate of today's church with its decadence, I am able to trace the source to a lack of prayer and fasting as the missing link. The preaching of the Word must be watered by prayer and fasting without which there can be no impact, no matter how effective we preach or how many volumes of books are written and read. II Corinthians 3:6 says, "Who also hath made us able ministers of the new testament; not of the letter, but of the spirit: for the letter killeth, but the spirit giveth life."

> The preaching of the Word must be watered by prayer and fasting without which there can be no impact.

Prayer and fasting will invoke and infuse the preached Word with the Spirit that brings the power and anointing, and this same Spirit will prepare hearts to receive the Word and transform lives. It is prayer and fasting that brings this enablement. It will restore the power, the miracles, healings, signs and wonders as Jesus promised. If we do not pray and fast, we cannot be effective in the ministry, and there would be no difference between those of the world and the body of Christ. As water keeps a plant alive, so does prayer and fasting keep our spirits alive.

In John 17:16, Jesus prayed, "They are not of the world,

even as I am not of the world," therefore, it is required of us that we be different from the world. The world's system is structured in such a way that unless we make a determination to get involved in or make time for prayer, a week may go by without us realizing that we have not had time to seek God in prayer. We seem to have time for every other thing such as work, shopping, T.V., movies, music and entertainment - everything except prayer.

For about twenty years I remained faithful to the Lord and sixteen of those years were before my marriage. I had sometimes been boastful of that, but when I relocated to a new environment, life was different and it was very hard to get by. I found myself hooked on my books and life's concerns both night and day. For the first time in many years, I had no time to pray or fast for days and weeks, and to my surprise, ungodly thoughts that would not easily come to my mind were running through freely. Since my circumstances made it difficult for me to commit myself to prayer, this trend of affairs was recurrent.

What else could be the missing link except prayer and fasting? I understood then that it was prayer and fasting that kept me through the years, and that for me to be victorious and walk as a conqueror I should never relegate prayer and fasting no matter what the circumstances. Zechariah 4:6b says, "Not by might, nor by power, but by my spirit, saith the Lord of hosts." There are numerous references in the New Testament about the need for prayer. After examining the following verses of Scripture on prayer and other related verses, I hope readers will be convinced that we cannot live our lives worthy of Christ without spending time in prayer.

Paul wrote to the church in Thessalonica:

- "Pray without ceasing" (1 Thessalonians 5:17).

- "But we will give ourselves continually to prayer, and to the ministry of the word" (Acts 6:4).

- "Let everyone who is godly pray..." (Psalm 32:6 NIV).

- Jesus said to His disciples, "Watch and pray so that you will not fall into temptation. The spirit is willing, but the body is weak" (Matthew 26:41 NIV).

- "But they that wait upon the Lord shall renew their strength; they shall mount up with wings as eagles; they shall run, and not be weary; and they shall walk, and not faint" (Isaiah 40:31).

- "Then Jesus told his disciples a parable to show them that they should always pray and not give up" (Luke 18:1 NIV).

All these verses confirm that prayer is our responsibility. Jesus Christ and the apostles could not do without prayer and we should emulate their example as followers do of their leaders. Prayer is the only channel by which we can draw closer to God and by it we will be able to live lives worthy of Christ. Paul addressed the saints in Ephesus thus, "Wherefore I also, after I heard of your faith in the Lord Jesus, and love unto all the saints, Cease not to give thanks for you, making mention of you in my prayers; That the God of our Lord Jesus Christ, the Father of glory, may give unto you the spirit of wisdom and revelation in the knowledge of him" (Ephesians 1:15-17).

From these Scriptural verses we find that prayer is an indispensable weapon in our Christian life and this cannot be overemphasized. Paul prayed for the saints so that they would know God better. In other words, to know God and walk in His precepts demands prayer, because it is prayer that brings the divine presence of God, His nature, His attitude, His characteristics, His righteousness, His power and His anointing which enables us to walk in obedience to His Word. God imparts His nature into us by His Spirit which gives us the enablement. There was an impartation from God to Moses after he had met with God on Mount Sinai. This explains why the Israelites could not look on the face of Moses (Exodus 34:29,30). For example, we all know too well that when we associate with people for a long time, we begin to exhibit some of their attributes. After associating with a friend of mine for a while, I realized that I was walking in the same manner that he used to walk.

The only way we can be like Christ is to relate with Him through prayer and His Word to enable Him to impart His nature into our lives. Without prayer we would die spiritually and the nature (holiness) and attitude of God could not become manifest in our lives.

PART TWO
Unveiling the Mystery of Prayer

Chapter 4

Unveiling the Mystery of Prayer

I believe that as the mystery of prayer and fasting is unveiled and unlocked, Christians will get a clearer understanding of the role that prayer plays in our Christian life and it will whet our appetite to pray and fast. Christians will then be the light that we are supposed to be. We will be the salt to preserve our communities, and we will be able to impact our world. In an attempt to discover the mystery of prayer and its paramount importance in our Christian journey, let us look at the definition of prayer from the New International Version and walk through a number of cases.

The New International Version of the Bible defines prayer as communication with God. Communication is a two-way street. It only occurs when there is a dialogue. We listen to God as much as we speak to Him in prayer. We can read the biographies and autobiographies of people and get to know them to a certain level but not intimately. Sometimes we may also know about people because someone might have told us about them. However, we cannot confidently say that we know the person until we talk to or communicate with them more frequently, have a personal contact or build a relationship with them. Your Pastor can teach and preach to you about God, but you can never know God until you develop a personal relationship with Him through prayer, fasting and the study of His Word.

From now on, we will use the words prayer and communication interchangeably.

Building a Relationship

Communication is basic to building any relationship, be it friendship, marriage, family or a business partnership. During communication there is a transfer or exchange of information and without it no relationship can succeed or survive. The more intense the communication, the more intimate and successful the relationship will be. It produces trust, respect, love, appreciation, acceptance, confidence, agreement, understanding and unites those who are involved in it. It stands to reason that if one is in a relationship and a need arises, the partner will automatically come to the aid of the one who is in need. For example, if you have a physician friend and you are in need of medical assistance, he or she will definitely come to your aid. If a friend of yours is an attorney, he will be of help with legal counsel in time of crisis.

What then happens when we communicate or talk to God on a regular basis? We build a strong relationship with God and He, being our Greatest Physician, will of necessity heal us of our infirmities when we fall sick. As our Chief Advocate, He will defend us when we have been falsely accused, or if we happen to be guilty, He forgives and helps us out. Oh! What a companion to have. For example, Jabez did not get up out of the blue and ask God for the enlargement of his territory and for God to bless him indeed. I believe he would have had a relationship with God before he could make such a request (I Chronicles 4:9). The language of his prayer suggests that he knew God and was known by God.

God is All in All, and if we are in a relationship with Him, He will come to our aid in our time of need. He is a Friend that sticks closer than a Brother (Proverbs 18:24b). He is our Father, our Physician, our Advocate, our Counselor, our Comforter, our Redeemer, our Savior, our Deliverer, our Provider and our source of everything. Prayer, therefore, no longer becomes asking and requesting from God only, but involves identifying with God and building a relationship with Him.

The Constancy of Prayer

In I Thessalonians 5:17, Paul admonishes believers to "pray without ceasing," or that we should "pray continually" (NIV). Why do we have to pray today, pray tomorrow and continue to pray day after day without ceasing? Is it not enough if we pray today and wait until the following week before we pray again?

Let us consider this; a husband talks to his wife today and does not talk to her tomorrow, the day after and on and on, and says that I will talk to my wife next week because I spoke to her yesterday. How would the wife feel about the relationship? A lot of questions will begin to run through her mind. It is obvious that all will not be well in the home. The marriage would definitely turn sour. We are obligated to talk to our spouses daily. This scenario will apply to our jobs as well. For example, if your boss or supervisor refuses to talk to you for a day or two, you will start to feel uncomfortable on the job. Likewise, we have to talk to God daily because we are the bride of Christ and we have to maintain and build our relationship with God daily through communication just as natural earthly relationships are built and maintained through communication. Talking to God is prayer which has to be on-going and never ending. It is our constancy in prayer that will bring us the victory. This explains why Paul admonishes us to pray without ceasing or that we should pray continually.

Our relationship with God also consists of studying His Word in order to know Him more and more and of giving God glory, honor, praise and rendering our service to Him in obedience. He created us for that purpose. In the course of time if a need arises, we should ask God for help because He can and He will. This is God's promise to us in Psalm 50:15 which says, "And call upon me in the day of trouble: I will deliver thee, and thou shalt glorify me."

Relationships are built through communication, and helping one another is also a part of relationships as has already been elaborated. We have a promise to be heirs of God and joint heirs with Christ (Romans 8:17). This can only be fulfilled if we make God our father through Christ by means of communication. Inheritance is a natural outcome of a relationship such as with a father and son or a husband and wife. All of these relationships are built through communication and as it is in the natural so it is in the spiritual. When we build a relationship with God, spiritual and material prosperity becomes our inheritance because we are joint heirs with Christ.

Following are some cases of negative and positive effects of communication that will help us to further unlock the mystery of prayer by revealing the extent to which communication can build relationships and unite people either for a good cause or for an evil cause as we sometimes experience in marriage, friendship and other forms of relationships. There are cases of people who were ruined or blessed as a result of communication and others describe how hundreds of souls were led to their destruction due to the influence of communication such as occurs in cults.

Although most of the incidents resulted in negative consequences, they will help to unlock the mystery and, therefore, the reason for the power of communication and for that matter the power of prayer. As you read through the cases, follow the

50

effects of communication in the episodes closely as the mystery of prayer is being unveiled.

Chapter 5

Husband and Wife

*I*n Paul's letter to the Church in Ephesus, he identifies the body of believers, the Church, as the bride of Christ just as a wife is to a husband (Ephesians 5:22-32). A marriage relationship has to be maintained through constant communication without which it cannot survive. Husbands and wives who live happily together for many years tend to have common interests. In most cases they have similar opinions and the reason for that lies in communication. As they share ideas, solve problems, reason together, correct one another and learn from each other, they tend to develop along the same lines and even have similar emotions in some cases. As the Bride of Christ, we have to maintain a constant link through communication in order to make our relationship with Christ successful.

When communication takes place between spouses over a period of time, there is a transference of thoughts, attributes or characteristics which is either shared or received from the other partner. For example, let us consider the episode of Ananias and Saphira from the Book of Acts.

"All the believers were one in heart and mind. No one claimed that any of his possessions was his own, but they shared everything they had. With great power the apostles continued to testify to the resurrection of the

Lord Jesus, and much grace was upon them all. There were no needy persons among them. For from time to time those who owned lands or houses sold them, brought the money from the sales and put it at the apostles' feet, and it was distributed to anyone as he had need. Joseph, a Levite from Cyprus, whom the apostles called Barnabas (which means Son of Encouragement), sold a field he owned and brought the money and put it at the apostles' feet" (Acts 4: 32-37 NIV).

"Now a man named Ananias, together with his wife Sapphira, also sold a piece of property. With his wife's full knowledge he kept back part of the money for himself, but brought the rest and put it at the apostles' feet. Then Peter said, 'Ananias, how is it that Satan has so filled your heart that you have lied to the Holy Spirit and have kept for yourself some of the money you received for the land? Didn't it belong to you before it was sold? And after it was sold, wasn't the money at your disposal? What made you think of doing such a thing? You have not lied to men but to God.' When Ananias heard this, he fell down and died. And great fear seized all who heard what had happened. Then the young men came forward, wrapped up his body, and carried him out and buried him" (Acts 5:1-6 NIV).

Sapphira came in a little while later, she told the same lies as her husband had and she also died in the manner of her husband (Acts 5:7-11). In this instance, communication had taken place between the couple and they were in agreement concerning the decision to tell a lie as Peter mentioned in verse 9 of Acts 5, "How is it that ye have agreed together to tempt the Spirit of the Lord?" We notice here that one of the outcomes of communication is agreement. Ananias and Sapphira lived under the dispensation of grace, but they perished because they agreed to tell lies. They spoke the same "language" because they had communicated.

Levels of Anointing

There are different levels of anointing and this is exemplified by Elisha asking Elijah to grant him a double portion of his anointing (II Kings 2:9). The Apostles seemingly had a higher level of anointing because of their commitment to prayer which made it possible for such demonstrations of power to be prevalent in their midst.

Many church folk tell lies, cheat, exploit, deceive and do all kinds of iniquities without any feeling of remorse. When one continues to disregard the convictions of the Holy Spirit, the heart becomes hardened and the person tends to live habitually in disobedience. Their conscience becomes seared with a hot iron and they are given over to reprobate minds (Romans 1:28). It looks like lying was the lifestyle of Ananias and Saphira and all grace had been exhausted and their cup was full, they were neither hot nor cold and God spewed them out of His mouth. Oh! What a tragedy that was. Ananias and Sapphira also lived under the dispensation of grace, so the question is "What was the difference between their era and ours?"

At the hour of prayer, Peter and John went to the beautiful gate and a lame man was expecting to receive from them. Then Peter said, "Silver and gold have I none; but such as I have give I thee: In the name of Jesus Christ of Nazareth rise up and walk. And he took him by the right hand, and lifted him up: and immediately his feet and ankle bones received strength" (Acts 3:6,7).

Why did the lame man receive healing immediately? Why do we not see these manifestations often these days?

Benny Hinn once said, "The Apostles did not have the silver and gold but they had the power. We have the silver and gold but lack the power". Why? Has God changed? No! Has His power diminished? No! What then made the difference? Remember that Acts 3:1 says, "At the hour of prayer" which means that the Apostles had set times devoted to prayer and the Word alone because they understood the importance and the role of prayer in their ministry and it was a daily devotion.

If we would give ourselves to prayer like our predecessors, we would start experiencing such "Acts" and believers would fear to live in any form of ungodliness.

Ananias and Sapphira, having lived together for many years and after the long years of communication, had developed the same ambition, common interest and, therefore, love of money. Ananias and Sapphira told the same lies at different times and suffered the same consequences. It was communication that brought about this catastrophe. Sapphira might not have been that covetous when she got married to Ananias and vice versa, but with time they had influenced each other through communication. Communication brought about a transformation and a change in their lives which led to a decision by both spouses to tell lies resulting in their destruction. If we could develop a strong relationship with God, our lives would be completely changed because we would be in agreement with God, speak His language and His power would work through us for His glory.

At any time in a marriage relationship, when there is a communication breakdown, the marriage is definitely headed for the rocks. The partners will drift towards different lines of thought and action, which may end up in a divorce. Just as communication brings agreement and unity, a breakdown in communication brings disagreement and disunity.

Lack of communication with God divorces us from Him, and we begin to live lives devoid of the spirituality that we derive from God through prayer. It is prayer that maintains our relationship with God and causes us to be in agreement with Him. We, being the bride of Christ, should not relinquish prayer if we are to develop and maintain our Christ likeness and for that matter our spirituality. Without prayer we will die spiritually as individuals and as a church and live on our own strength. However, the old saying goes that "the arm of flesh will fail us." This means that when we pray continually we develop common interests with God, we share common ideas with Him, we tend to live in agreement and we more or less develop the mind of Christ (I Corinthians 2:16).

> **It is prayer that maintains our relationship with God and causes us to be in agreement with Him.**

Any group of believers or church which does not commit to prayer and fasting is an entertainment organization or center because the power of believers and the church is obtained through prayer, fasting and the study of the Word. It does not matter the size of the congregation, it is the presence of God that dwells in the midst of His people that matters (I Chronicles 7:1,2). You cannot study the Word without prayer and you cannot pray without studying the Word. The two go together. One is incomplete without the other. These are the two lines of communication given to us by God.

Chapter 6

What Was God Thinking?

*H*ow does God feel about the power of communication? One may wonder, how can you know the mind of God? There is an interesting account in the Book of Genesis which reveals God's thoughts about communication.

"Now the whole world had one language and a common speech. As men moved eastward, they found a plain in Shinar and settled there. They said to each other, 'Come, let's make bricks and bake them thoroughly.' They used brick instead of stone, and tar for mortar. Then they said, 'Come, let us build ourselves a city, with a tower that reaches to the heavens, so that we may make a name for ourselves and not be scattered over the face of the whole earth.' But the Lord came down to see the city and the tower that the men were building. The Lord said, 'If as one people speaking the same language they have begun to do this, then nothing they plan to do will be impossible for them. Come, let us go down and confuse their language so they will not understand each other.' So the Lord scattered them from there over all the earth, and they stopped building the city. That is why it was called Babel - because there the Lord confused the language of the whole world. From there the Lord scattered them over the face of the whole earth" (Genesis 11:1-9 NIV).

Some questions begin to run through one's mind as this story unfolds. The first is, Why did God change their language? And the second is, What is in the communication that drew God's attention to what they proposed to do?

1.   Apparently God changed their language to prevent communication among the people of Shinar.

2.   One of the effects of communication is that it brings unity which results in strength and power. Wherever there is unity of purpose, a lot could be accomplished either for good or evil.

They wanted to build a tower that would reach to heaven in order to make a name and bring glory to themselves, but God will not share His glory with any man. He said "I am the Lord; that is my name! I will not give my glory to another or my praise to idols" (Isaiah 42:8 NIV). In this unique story, God saw that men had rebelled against Him in their hearts and He knew that they could accomplish their evil desires through communication. As the Creator, He thought that if He did not react immediately men would oppose His authority due to the fact that they were becoming powerful and strong as a result of their unity through communication. God decided to "fight" back by eliminating their medium of communication, because if men were united through a common language, then nothing would be impossible for them. God was moved by the unity of the people and felt "threatened" and He decided to react immediately because they could accomplish their evil desires as long as they remained united. The saying goes that "In unity lies strength." We see here the power and effect of unity in demonstration, but the unity was being abused and misused by the people of Shinar.

If Christians could understand each other and unite based on the fact that the Bible says in I Corinthians 12:5 that, "There are differences of administrations, but the same Lord," there is nothing that we could not accomplish for the Kingdom.

There are many ways that God could have addressed the problem in Shinar. For instance, He could have pulled down the tower, but He chose to confuse their medium of communication which was the real threat and which would address the problem at its root. God knows the inherent power of communication, and therefore, He changed their language and prevented them from achieving their objective.

From this incident the power of communication becomes very evident. As we communicate with God, we tend to develop a unity of purpose, we also share in His strength and power and are able to accomplish a lot for His Kingdom. There is definitely "something" in communication that could pose a "threat" to the throne of a Sovereign and Almighty God. In other words, it drew the attention of the creator Himself.

Can you imagine what damage, havoc or wreckage we would cause the kingdom of Satan if Christians could unite in a mega-prayer and fasting at least once every year like the fasting that was declared by Queen Esther in the Assyrian Kingdom for the deliverance of the Jews during the threat of annihilation by Haman? Three days of intensive, determined and rigorous mega-prayer and fasting by all believers around the globe would turn the tide and the course of history. People who convert to Christianity are threatened with death or imprisonment in some parts of Asia, Sudan and other parts of the world. Threats of terrorism and pestilence such as cancer and AIDS that have brought misery to humankind are all signs of the return of our Lord and Master Jesus Christ. These diseases are trying to exalt themselves above the name of our Lord Jesus. The mention of these names bring fear to the very elect. Let us arise and fight the good fight of faith against the evil spirits behind these diseases. The devil has confused and torn down the unity of Christians with mere differences of administrations and doctrinal emphasis.

If the people of Shinar could unite for an evil course, then we can also unite for a just course for the good of the Kingdom and to the glory of God.

We have all been born into One Lord, One Faith and One Baptism. We have all been redeemed by the same blood. Rick Warren wrote, "Today's culture of independent individualism has created many spiritual orphans - "bunny believers" who hop around from one church to another without any identity, accountability, or commitment." He went on to say, "When we come together in love as a church family from different backgrounds, race, and social status, it is a powerful witness to the world. You are not the body of Christ on your own. You need others to express that. Together, not separated, we are His Body."

Chapter 7

Friendship

*A*ristotle had this to say about friendship: "Beast knows beast; birds of the same feathers flock together." Cervantes also said, "Tell me what company thou keepest, and I'll tell thee what thou art." Susanne Hinn, wife of Evangelist Benny Hinn, said rightly "You are known by the people you avoid." King Solomon, the wisest man that ever lived said in Proverbs 22:24,25a "Make no friendship with an angry man; and with a furious man thou shalt not go: Lest thou learn his ways."

Friendship has the potential to build people up or ruin them. Many people have been caught up in the web of friendships from which they found it difficult to break free. Sometimes people become addicted to a myriad of habits due to the friends with whom they associate. Teenagers especially fall victims to such associations. Children who have been brought up in Christian homes may find themselves going wayward because of bad associations. Many of us have at one time or another found ourselves caught up in relationships that have influenced our lives greatly. The Bible is replete with many examples of friendship.

Shadrach, Meshach and Abednego

Friendship does not always produce negative results; sometimes it yields good fruits. Let us consider the fascinating account of three friends, Shadrach, Meshach and Abednego found in Daniel 3:12-18:

> "'But there are some Jews whom you have set over the affairs of the province of Babylon — Shadrach, Meshach and Abednego — who pay no attention to you, O king. They neither serve your gods nor worship the image of gold you have set up.' Furious with rage, Nebuchadnezzar summoned Shadrach, Meshach and Abednego. So these men were brought before the king, and Nebuchadnezzar said to them, 'Is it true, Shadrach, Meshach and Abednego, that you do not serve my gods or worship the image of gold I have set up? Now when you hear the sound of the horn, flute, zither, lyre, harp, pipes and all kinds of music, if you are ready to fall down and worship the image I made, very good. But if you do not worship it, you will be thrown immediately into a blazing furnace. Then what god will be able to rescue you from my hand?' Shadrach, Meshach and Abednego replied to the king, 'O Nebuchadnezzar, we do not need to defend ourselves before you in this matter. If we are thrown into the blazing furnace, the God we serve is able to save us from it, and he will rescue us from your hand, O king. But even if he does not, we want you to know, O king, that we will not serve your gods or worship the image of gold you have set up'" (NIV).

The King was outraged and ordered that the three friends be thrown into a blazing furnace. The God of Shadrach, Meshach and Abednego sent an angel into the furnace to protect them and their bodies were not harmed (Daniel 3:19-27 NIV).

"Then Nebuchadnezzar said, 'Praise be to the God of
Shadrach, Meshach and Abednego, who has sent his
angel and rescued his servants! They trusted in him and
defied the king's command and were willing to give up
their lives rather than serve or worship any god except
their own God. Therefore I decree that the people of
any nation or language who say anything against the
God of Shadrach, Meshach and Abednego be cut into
pieces and their houses be turned into piles of rubble,
for no other god can save in this way.' Then the king
promoted Shadrach, Meshach and Abednego in the
province of Babylon" (Daniel 3:28-30 NIV).

The three friends, Shadrach, Meshach and Abednego,
held prominent positions within the Babylonian government.
Because they refused to bow down to a golden idol, they were
condemned to a fiery death but God intervened and spared their
lives. These friends had developed the same faith, boldness
and confidence in God through communication because they
reasoned together, prayed to God, and, therefore, were able
to stand firm for God without compromise. They had become
"birds of the same feathers" and were ready to die for their faith.
Communication had produced unity of thought, action, faith,
boldness and confidence in the God of Israel. They were firm in
their convictions, uncompromising in their resolve, stood for the
truth and were bonded to God and to each other.

As said earlier on, communication can develop the
character of people either in positive or negative ways. On 9/11
nineteen educated, intelligent and progressive terrorists were
bold, united and agreed to die in order to destroy lives and
property because they had communicated.

The Lords of Chaos

In a two-hour Dateline NBC/Court TV Special which aired on March 15, 2002, Keith Morrison looked at three friends that were about to graduate from high school who turned from young boys to killers in a matter of weeks. The Lords of Chaos and the leader of their gang, Kevin Foster, were eventually convicted for the murder of their teacher. Jim Greenhill, a crime reporter in Fort Myers, Florida, who was covering the Lords of Chaos met frequently with Kevin Foster who was then on Florida's Death Row. They became friends and had many moments together.

Jim visited Kevin frequently and they exchanged letters on a regular basis. After winning the confidence of Jim, Kevin hoping to get a new trial, solicited Jim to murder three of the witnesses against him with the assistance of Kevin's mother, Ruby Foster. Jim had purchased himself a gun and went on shooting adventures at the back of his house. He became obsessed with a desire to use his gun. Kevin also had a list of names of people who were involved in his trial to be murdered after his release including Jim Greenhill's wife who was a photographer.

Jim Greenhill, a sympathizer of Kevin had received a gun from Ruby Foster who explained that the gun was not registered and should be used for the murder. The plan which would be used to carry out the murder had been put in place. Jim Greenhill by heaven's intervention went to prosecutors instead and they enlisted him as a confidential informant.

This story proves that communication has a transforming power. Jim was carrying out his normal duties as a writer but communication being his main tool of operation got the edge of him and almost changed him into a murderer. Kevin and his mother Ruby were charged with conspiracy to commit first-degree murder and are awaiting trial. An innocent man was almost turned into an evil and murderous person but the opposite is also possible. An evil person can be transformed into a good person through communication and for that matter communication with God changes the hearts of sinners. The cases cited so far show that wherever there has been communication a change or transformation has taken place. Friendship with God will make us all that He created us to be. It will develop our potential to its maximum.

Chapter 8

Leader and Followers

$\mathscr{T}$he following are excerpts of two incidents involving cult leaders who were able to enslave hundreds of people and led them to their destruction through communication.

The People's Temple

In 1978, 913 followers of the People's Temple committed a mass suicide in northern Guyana at a site called Jonestown. The charismatic leader of Jonestown was Jim Jones, a preacher who set up the People's Temple in San Francisco and ultimately moved his followers to a more clandestine site in Guyana.

While Jones was preaching in San Francisco, he helped out many local and even national campaigns and was even seen as a leader with much power in the community. However, once he had all of his members in Jonestown his personality changed. Away from the constraints of American soil, Jonestown and its members became very cultish. Jones heightened regulations on his followers and their engagement to the sect. Eventually, Jones began to claim his true divinity. "Jones, for example, now claimed to be the reincarnation of Jesus, as well as Ikhnaton, Buddha, Lenin and Father Divine." Paranoia and complete control became Jones personality, once he obtained such a close-knit group.

As time went on, Jones began to stage rehearsals of his eventual mass suicide plan that he would ultimately enact. These activities called "white nights" began with sirens going off in the middle of the night and none of the members of Jonestown would know if it were real or not. "A mass meeting would ensue — they would be told that the jungle was swarming with mercenaries — they were given a small glass of red liquid to drink. They were told that the liquid contained poison and that they would die within 45 minutes. They all did as they were told" (Ganter 1989).

In 1978, U.S. Congressman Leo Ryan went to Jonestown to investigate supposed abuses by the People's Temple of its members who had decided to deflect. Realizing this, Jones ordered him killed, which was done. Sensing his utopia in the jungle would surely come to an end after word got back to the States about Ryan, Jones decided to put his suicide plan into action. He told his subjects that it was a "revolutionary death." He had a large quantity of fruit punch laced with cyanide. After making all 276 children of Jonestown drink the punch, all the adults followed suit, after which Jones apparently killed himself with a gunshot to the head. In all it was reported that 914 people had died.

In this bizarre story of the People's Temple, we find that communication has an inherent power to transform people's lives either for good or evil. Complete control became the personality of Reverend Jim Jones of the People's Temple. How could so many people be misled to the extent of dying for someone who was as human and as needy as they were? How could someone's mind be controlled and influenced by another person, to an extent that one could sacrifice his or her life for such an unjustifiable cause?

The secret lies in communication through which many

minds have been influenced, controlled, dominated or enslaved so much that dying for an unjust cause becomes very easy. Think of current terrorist activities around the world. Communication has made into suicide bombers men and women who could have had a better future but instead were made into human bombs through the weapon of communication.

The leader had communicated much to his followers and they had the same beliefs and ideas and had developed the same mind set. They saw and understood things in the same way, reasoned along the same lines and, therefore, agreed to carry out a disastrous act. This episode shows clearly the inherent power of communication, a power destructively abused by Jim Jones.

Let no man deceive you with vain words because no man died for you, no pastor died for you, no church was crucified for you. Jesus alone paid the price for our salvation. Jesus paid the debt that we owe, because we owed the debt that we could not pay. Like Paul said, even if an angel from heaven bring any other doctrine different from what you have been taught let him be accursed (Galatians 1:8).

Heaven's Gate

On March 26, 1998 in a luxurious mansion at Rancho Santa Fe near San Diego in California in the United States, police found 39 bodies of members of the Heaven's Gate, another religious organization. Their ages varied from teenagers to elderly. They included an Ex-Miss Rodeo, a former cowboy movie actor, and the brother of an actress in the TV series Star Trek. Some of them were castrated. This was an extreme case of negative ideas about sex, which one may find also elsewhere in occultism, such as in the novel 'The Celestine Prophecy' by James Redfield. They wore uniforms and after their deaths, purple shrouds were used to cover them.

71

The American paranormal spoon-bender, Uri Geller, known from TV entertainment shows in the Netherlands and elsewhere, said on CNN television that he might have been among the members of the Heaven's Gate cult who died. A friend had asked him to join the cult. However, Uri did not join even though he too, believed in flying saucers. He said he did not like the idea of giving up all his earthly possessions to Heaven's Gate leader, Marshall Herff Applewhite upon joining.

The Heaven's Gate members had paid for their obedience to Applewhite, Jesus would reincarnate according to them after death. Applewhite himself compared the obedience of a good religious disciple to that of a good dog. Applewhite had told them that he would soon die of cancer (according to the coroners postmortem, he did not have cancer at all). If his devotees would follow him into death, a UFO, supposed to accompany the Hale-Bopp comet, would come and take them.

Alan Hale, discoverer of the Hale-Bopp Comet said that Heaven's Gate members had bought an expensive telescope to observe the UFO's. However, they returned it to the shop saying it was defective. "Why is it defective?" the shopkeeper asked. "One cannot see the UFO with it!" Just before the festival of Easter signifying the resurrection of Jesus from the dead, according to Christianity, the UFO would take them to reincarnation on another planet. There they would see Bonnie Nettles again, the movement's co-founder, who they believed had really died of cancer. Those who doubted were referred to the Christian Bible book of Revelations chapter eleven where John saw a vision of the resurrection of the dead and heard a loud voice from heaven saying to them, "Come up here" and they went up to heaven in a cloud. In his farewell message on video, Applewhite expressed his solidarity with the cults of David Koresh and the Order of the Solar Temple. They also had been willing to follow their shepherd's, their leaders, into the hereafter."

The devotees of Applewhite would follow him to death and gave up all their earthly possessions to their leader upon joining the Heaven's Gate because they were convinced of what Applewhite had related to them. After many years of toil to acquire possessions, the leader of Heaven's Gate was able to convince them to give up their possessions. The power of communication has been abused by many leaders to the detriment of their followers.

When Jesus Christ was preparing to go to the cross, it was a very trying moment for Him. He requested that if it be possible the cup should be taken away from Him. He prayed three times saying the same words (Matthew 26:39-44). Jesus was in agony and prayed earnestly and his sweat was as great drops of blood (Luke 22:44). From all indications, death was not an easy assignment for Jesus Christ. He struggled through prayer looking for a way of escape, but the persistent communication with God helped Him to go to the cross with the help of an angel sent by God (Luke 22:42,43). The followers of Applewhite however, had no difficulty believing their leader and dying with him because of the power of communication.

Leaders usually have the power to influence the minds of their followers through communication and, therefore, their perceptions and decisions are affected by the leader. This is the reason Paul admonishes us that, "I exhort therefore, that, first of all, supplications, prayers, intercessions, and giving of thanks, be made for all men; For kings, and for all that are in authority; that we may lead a quiet and peaceable life in all godliness and honesty" I Timothy 2:1,2. The primary thing is to intercede for leaders even before our personal needs because we all shall be at risk if we are misled by our leaders.

Chapter 9

Teacher and Students

$\mathscr{T}$he Bible records in the Book of Acts 4:13, "When they saw the courage of Peter and John and realized that they were unschooled, ordinary men, they were astonished and they took note that these men had been with Jesus" (NIV). As unlearned as the apostles were, they had been schooled in the teachings of their master. They understood the Bible; they had power, authority and anointing because they sat at the feet of Jesus Christ.

When students sit at the feet of their teacher, a time comes when they develop mentally and attain the level of their teacher intellectually and as it does happen sometimes they may develop beyond the level of their teacher. As the teacher teaches and students ask questions, information is passed on and exchanged. The teacher and student progress toward a common perspective due to the communication that has taken place. The following account in the book of Acts also reveals what was accomplished when communication took place between Barnabas, Saul and those who believed in Christ.

> "News of this reached the ears of the church at Jerusalem, and they sent Barnabas to Antioch. When he arrived and saw the evidence of the grace of God, he was glad and encouraged them all to remain true to the Lord with all their hearts. He was a good man, full

of the Holy Spirit and faith, and a great number of people were brought to the Lord. Then Barnabas went to Tarsus to look for Saul, and when he found him, he brought him to Antioch. So for a whole year Barnabas and Saul met with the church and taught great numbers of people. The disciples were called Christians first at Antioch" (Acts 11:22-25 NIV).

The disciples believed and trusted in the Lord Jesus Christ and when Saul and Barnabas taught their followers the Word of God daily for a whole year, their world view was changed. They began to reason in the same way as their teachers, spoke the things of God, and acted like Christ. They were transformed from the kingdom of darkness into the kingdom of light. The things they loved and cherished before were relegated and abandoned, and they literally lived their lives as their Master Jesus Christ and were identified and called Christians by onlookers and those who knew them. Communication brought about a change of character and attitude. The disciples developed a Christian character because their teachers communicated Christian principles to them.

The need for prayer in the life of a child of God cannot be overemphasized. Jesus Christ promised the disciples that they would do the same works He was doing, and they could do greater works than He did because He was going to the Father (John 14:12). Jesus gave the disciples the opportunity to learn more and develop beyond His level through communication as it does happen sometimes with students and their teacher.

Robert Coleman wrote, "Jesus expected the men he was with to obey him. They were not required to be smart, but they had to be loyal. This became the distinguishing mark by which they were known. They were called his "disciples" meaning that they were "learners" or "pupils" of the Master... although it was inevitable, for in time obedient followers invariably take on the character of their leader." Exchange of information takes place between a teacher and his or her students which produces growth in knowledge of the subject or area of communication. The student later on develops the same mindset as the teacher and in time their perceptions become affected and changed. It is interesting to know that the student may even be affected by the teacher's nature and sometimes his gestures. Communication, therefore, develops the character of individuals either in a positive or negative way.

NOTES:

PART THREE
Unlocking the Mystery of Prayer

Chapter 10

Unlocking the Mystery of Prayer

*I*n all the cases cited, communication led to a transformation, a turn around, a change of mind which sometimes had devastating effects. Indeed, communication can lead to enslavement, bondage, domination, brainwashing and control. It could also lead to knowledge and deliverance with its accompanying liberty and freedom. Communication with God also has effects, but the difference is that with God it always yields positive results. The question to grapple with is, "What is in communication that causes these effects?"

Words are Spirits

In Genesis 1:3 it is written, "God said, let there be light and there was light." Until God spoke there was no manifestation. From the story of creation we know that God created the world with the words of His mouth, therefore, words have a creative ability. Everything in this world was spoken into existence by the creative power of God's Word except man who was molded by God from the dust of the earth in His image and likeness. God has given that same creative ability to mankind and we may also use it to build or destroy.

People die but their spoken or written words continue to live and they can always be quoted from generation to generation.

Martin Luther King, Jr. is always remembered by his "I Have a Dream" speech. President George Bush said in his last state of the union address that "People compete for votes and cooperate for results." This statement will be remembered for ever. Other leaders, past and present have made statements decades ago which are still being quoted. Our grandparents, mothers and fathers have said things that will never be forgotten. The reason why words do not die is found in John 6:63b, where Jesus said, "The words that I speak unto you, they are spirit, and they are life."

There is a force or a spirit behind words. This force is either good or evil and can create, build, bless, destroy or bring curses. Solomon, the wisest man who has ever walked the face of this earth said, "Death and life are in the power of the tongue: and they that love it shall eat the fruit thereof" (Proverbs 18:21). It is the spirit, power and creative ability behind the words which God speaks to us that causes change in our lives. It gives us life through faith, hope, joy, peace, comfort and all the blessings that come with God's words. When we pray to God, He communicates back to us through His Word, through people, dreams, visions, soul (mind), angels and Holy Spirit (Inner Man) or a "still small voice." He may speak face to face as He did with Moses through His divine means (Exodus 33:11) (explained in more detail in Chapter Thirty-One, "How Does God Talk Back to Us?").

The Penetrative Power of Words

It is written in Hebrews 4:12, "For the word of God is quick, and powerful, and sharper than any two-edged sword, piercing even to the dividing asunder of soul and spirit, and of the joints and marrow, and is a discerner of the thoughts and intents of the heart." The Word of God can cut, pierce and is capable of breaking loose the hardness in the hearts of men. It can discern all the thoughts and all the positive and negative intents and secret desires of men. These capabilities of God's Word make it efficient in addressing issues in the lives of men and women, it can cleanse, purify, liberate and set captives free, thereby, bringing change and transformation in the lives of people.

Jesus sent His Word to heal because His Word is quick, powerful and sharp, has no boundaries, and unlike ballistic missiles, cannot be intercepted; it is spirit and has life. This explains why we can pray by proxy and expect the Word to function wherever it is sent. In the gospel of Matthew 8:8 it is written, "The centurion answered and said, Lord, I am not worthy that thou shouldest come under my roof: but speak the word only, and my servant shall be healed." The centurion believed that Jesus Word had power to accomplish whatever it is meant to accomplish and he saw the manifestation in his servant's healing. When God communicates to us His Word having creativity, spirit, life, being quick and powerful, sharper than any two-edged sword, the Word brings healing, deliverance and restoration. It gives wisdom, makes us courageous, brings the anointing of God upon us and gives us power for service. It is the source of all our breakthroughs both in the spirit and in the natural.

The Magnetic Power of Words

"A good man out of the good treasure of his heart bringeth forth that which is good; and an evil man out of the evil treasure of his heart bringeth forth that which is evil: for of the abundance of the heart his mouth speaketh" (Luke 6:45). What is in a man is that which comes out of him. "For as he thinketh in his heart, so *is* he" (Proverbs 23:7a).

Communication is one of the means by which spirits can be transferred from one person to the other. When we speak to people, the spirit behind the words with its concomitant power is passed on. When the spirit is good, the individual begins to manifest the fruits of that spirit. On the other hand when the spirit is evil, the fruits of evil will begin to manifest. For example, a man says to a woman, "I am in love with you." After interacting with the woman for some time, those words begin to work on the mind (soul) of the lady. It then transfers from her mind to her heart (spirit) and later the whole body (flesh) of the woman becomes obsessed with the feeling of love and affection towards the man. She begins to think about it day and night and even starts dreaming about it, talks to others about what the man had told her. Before long her body becomes electrified with a current of love flowing through. The current magnetizes her body and creates a magnetic effect. She then becomes attracted to the man and draws close to him. Then comes a time when the two become attached to one another and eventually may lead to them "tying the knot" and becoming one flesh.

The Negative Effect of Words

When this same woman starts bringing forth children, her body changes, she may grow bigger and in the event of an argument, her husband might get "pissed off" and call the woman, "You fat B." These words capture the woman's mind and then descend to her heart. Her body becomes obsessed with anger which runs through her body like electrical currents. Now the current demagnetizes her body of the affection and love she had for her husband and she begins to withdraw from the man and eventually this could lead to a divorce.

The reason why words have electrical, magnetic, domineering, obsessive and controlling ability is found again in the words of Jesus in John 6:63: "Words are spirit, and they are life." When we communicate with God, His Word penetrates our soul, spirit and body. His Word electrifies and magnetizes us, brings healing to us, hope, courage, comfort, peace and tranquility because of the spirit in His Word.

The Power of the Word

What makes God's Word powerful, magnetic and penetrative is that God stands behind His Word. God is in His Word and God is His Word and His Word is God according to John 1:1. God and His word are inseparable. The power in God's Word is demonstrated in the centurion's account and also in the story of the nobleman in the gospel of John 4:46-53 which says:

"So Jesus came again into Cana of Galilee, where he made the water wine. And there was a certain nobleman, whose son was sick at Capernaum. When he heard that Jesus was come out of Judaea into Galilee, he went unto him, and besought him that he would come down, and heal his son: for he was at the point of death. Then Jesus said unto him, Except ye see signs and wonders, ye will not believe. The nobleman saith unto him, Sir, come down ere my child die. Jesus saith unto him, Go thy way; thy son liveth. And the man believed the word that Jesus had spoken unto him, and he went his way. And as he was now going down, his servants met him, and told *him*, saying, Thy son liveth. Then enquired he of them the hour when he began to amend. And they said unto him, Yesterday at the seventh hour the fever left him. So the father knew that *it was* at the same hour, in the which Jesus said unto him, Thy son liveth: and himself believed, and his whole house."

When Jesus answered "thy son liveth," that concluded the whole matter because the spoken Word was life, was spirit and it was God. What Jesus did was He invoked God Himself into the son's condition and sickness had no choice but to flee. The Word has no boundaries, is not limited by distance and cannot be hindered because it is God.

Transference of Spirits

God's heart abounds with goodness and out of that treasure He speaks and brings forth nothing short of goodness to us and we in turn bring forth good fruit. God transfers His Spirit to us through His Words as we communicate with Him.

Husband and Wife

No one knows whether Ananias or Saphira had an abundance of lies or covetousness in their hearts, but as they communicated each day out of their abundance there was transference of spirits, they agreed and, therefore, had a common goal. "Can two walk together, except they be agreed?" (Amos 3:3). Although they were questioned at different times, they told the same lies. They had become "birds of the same feathers" as a result of communication, and they suffered an unfortunate consequence.

What Was God Thinking?

God knew this "secret" when He reacted to the common language of the people in Shinar who decided to build a tower reaching to heaven. It is astonishing to hear God's comment, "If as one people speaking the same language they have begun to do this, then nothing they plan to do will be impossible for them" (Genesis 11:6 NIV).The fact that God decided to confuse their medium of communication is an attestation that communication has an inherent power. People can accomplish a lot when they become united through communication. God could have destroyed the tower but He chose to destroy their unity by confusing their language because their communication was the real "threat."

Friendship

The three friends, Shadrach, Meshach and Abednego, were not fearful, they were full of courage, they were uncompromising and they were firm in their resolve as a result of their communication with God and with each other.

From the story, "The Lords of Chaos," as narrated, friendship is one of the devil's powerful weapons. Peer pressure among teenagers is an especially powerful tool in the hands of the devil. Parents must, therefore, be watchful of their children's associates. Robert Durham, principal of Riverdale High School in Fort Myers, Florida, commenting on the Lords of Chaos had this to say, "The Lords didn't fit the mold of bad boys. They did all the things parents expect them to do. These could be anyone's kids."

It is obvious that Jim Greenhill, the writer of the story on the "Lords of Chaos," was influenced by the evil words that were communicated from Kevin Foster who was the mastermind of the murders. An adage goes that "a bad company destroys good manners." This is exactly what happened to Jim because of the evil, creative and transforming power that was behind Kevin's communication.

A friend of ours intimated to us that her parents refused to allow her to keep company with certain kinds of friends when she was growing up as a teenager. It was difficult for her to accommodate that during those times. Now she is an attorney and recalls how many of those girls became pregnant and dropped out of school. Her parents were right.

Leader and Followers

In the cults described, the followers had a similar experience. They were transformed to the point of willingness to die for an unjust cause because of communication between them and their leader.

Teacher and Student

A Physics teacher like any other subject teacher makes physicists out of his students through communication; likewise, a disciple of Christ also makes disciples out of his students through communication. The teacher's heart and mind is full of what he believes and stands for. In the end, he transfers his knowledge or his ideas to his students, and they become like their teacher.

Volumes of books have been written on prayer and people are always talking about this subject. The apostles gave themselves to prayer. Jesus who was God incarnate lived a life of prayer. One may wonder, "What is in prayer that makes it so dear to God's heart?" There is indeed something in prayer to be desired.

In all the cases cited, people's lives were transformed either for good or bad. Association with God through prayer and study of His Word, will transform our lives in a positive way because His Spirit, His power, His nature or attributes are transferred into our lives.

E. M. Bounds wrote, "Prayer is simply faith resting in, acting with, leaning on, and obeying God. This is why God loves it so well, why He puts all power into its hands, and why He so highly esteems people of prayer."

Chapter 11

In Unity with God

*J*esus said, "...I do nothing on my own but speak just what the Father has taught me" (John 8:28b NIV). Jesus Christ communed with the Father and became one with Him. He only spoke what God had communicated into His spirit. He told the disciples "I and the Father are one" (John 10:30 NIV). God communicates out of the abundance of His heart. He communicates faith, hope, joy, peace, love, healing, holiness, humility, patience, mercy, wisdom, knowledge, liberty, power, anointing and boldness. His nature and glory also comes upon us (Exodus 34:29-30).

Jesus said in Matthew 11:29b, "...learn from me, for I am gentle and humble in heart..." (NIV). Paul wrote, "For this reason I am sending to you Timothy, my son whom I love, who is faithful in the Lord. He will remind you of my way of life in Christ Jesus, which agrees with what I teach everywhere in every church" (I Corinthians 4:17 NIV). Jesus and Paul could confidently say that we should learn from them because they have been with God through prayer and that is the reason they were so effective in their ministries. God lived His life through them because of their commitment to prayer and the study of His Word. As God transferred the abundance of His heart to them through prayer and His Word, they became one with Him. This resulted in the fruit of the Spirit manifesting in their lives.

If we communicate with God, we would experience the same kind of transformation. People will call us Christians or followers of Christ like the people of Antioch, because we have been with the Lord in prayer and have been united with Him.

Receiving the Anointing

God did extraordinary miracles by the hand of Paul. Handkerchiefs and aprons that had touched him were taken to the sick, their illnesses were cured and the evil spirits left them (Acts 19:11,12).

> "Some Jews who went around driving out evil spirits tried to invoke the name of the Lord Jesus over those who were demon-possessed. They would say, 'In the name of Jesus, whom Paul preaches, I command you to come out.' Seven sons of Sceva, a Jewish chief priest, were doing this. One day the evil spirit answered them, 'Jesus I know, and I know about Paul, but who are you?' Then the man who had the evil spirit jumped on them and overpowered them all. He gave them such a beating that they ran out of the house naked and bleeding" (Acts 19:13-16 NIV).

The seven sons of Sceva could not cast out the demons because they had not communicated with God in order to receive the anointing and the power to perform such a task. It is God's Spirit and anointing that enabled the Apostles to do the miraculous and the only way they could receive this impartation was through prayer. They paid the price by spending time with God to receive the anointing and the power for the great commission.

God communicates His Words into our spirits thereby making our words also become powerful like God's Words and enabling us to overcome the devil. Our words are made creative like God's Words and according to the will of God our prayers are answered. The Word of God says in John 15:7, "If you remain in me and my words remain in you, ask whatever you wish, and it will be given you" (NIV). Through prayer, God's Words begin to dwell and remain in us. We are able to remain in Him and through that unity of purpose, God will speak through us because His Word abides in us.

Jesus was victorious because He committed Himself to prayer. "How God anointed Jesus of Nazareth with the Holy Ghost and with power: who went about doing good, and healing all that were oppressed of the devil; for God was with him" (Acts 10:38 KJV). The Apostles were also victorious, because they followed the footsteps of their master, for they said, "We will give our attention to prayer and the ministry of the word" (Acts 6:4 NIV). What else could let the power of God rest upon us to make us victorious besides prayer and our obedience to His Word?

Clifton Jones wrote, "There is no other way on planet earth that anointing can be obtained. There is absolutely nothing that can take its place. No, not talent, human knowledge, man's wisdom, beautiful robes, highly learned principles, nor promotion to a higher office. None of the above, or any of their relatives, can take the place of anointing purchased by prayer."

As we commune with God, He talks back to us and His Word transforms, changes and turns our lives around by the creative power and force that is behind His Words. He imparts His anointing, power, wisdom and knowledge to us to enable us to live Godly lives and do His work. When we pray, we invoke the presence of God into our lives. He promised to be with us unto the end of the world. He walks and talks with us and we share in His thoughts, and we tend to live in agreement and unity with Him, just as it happens with husbands and wives, friends, teachers and students and leaders and their followers. To sum it all up, we become "birds of the same feathers with God" as a result of communication with Him.

Chapter 12

Why the Need for Prayer?

The need for prayer cannot be over emphasized. God is the source of our strength and Scripture also lets us know that, "In whose hand *is* the soul of every living thing, and the breath of all mankind" (Job 12:10). This verse shows evidently that we cannot do or achieve anything in our own strength or power. Jesus declared in John 15:5, "I am the vine, ye are the branches: He that abideth in me, and I in him, the same bringeth forth much fruit: for without me ye can do nothing." When we fellowship with God in prayer, we come out knowing that our sins have been forgiven; we become empowered with His strength, anointing and His wisdom to help us in our daily lives.

When we study the life of Jesus Christ, we learn that He did not do anything without first consulting with God. He received His anointing, strength and direction from God through prayer. We also know from Scripture that prayer is a command to be obeyed. If we neglect prayer, we become disobedient to God.

God wants to have a relationship with all His children as He did with Jesus Christ, and this can only be achieved through communication. The advice and guidance we receive, and the strength we derive from God through prayer will enable us to overcome temptation and be able to stand in the evil day. The

Bible declares, "Then he returned to his disciples and found them sleeping. 'Could you men not keep watch with me for one hour?' he asked Peter. 'Watch and pray so that you will not fall into temptation. The spirit is willing, but the body is weak'" (Matthew 26:40,41 NIV). We glean from this verse that Jesus expects us to spend time in prayer in order to keep us strong in the spirit and to receive guidance from God to overcome temptations. Since we were made from the dust of the earth, we always want to do earthly things, which is opposed to the things of the spirit because the flesh (body) is weak. We need God's strength and power to be able to bring the flesh under submission and live and walk in the Spirit and bear fruits of the Spirit.

It is only through prayer that God would have a place in and impact our lives. Jesus prayed and taught us how to pray; the apostles prayed and wrote that "men ought always to pray, and not to faint" (Luke 18:1). God created us for fellowship and union through communication as is exemplified in the Garden of Eden (Genesis 2:18). We have heard that men who have been used mightily of God both dead and alive spent long hours (quality time) communicating with Him in order to be effective. We now know the secret of their anointing and power in their ministries.

If an association with fellow human beings such as spouses, friends, teachers, students, leaders and followers can impact one's life, will not an association with God impact our lives so much more? Herein lies the secret of the mystery of prayer. This is the reason why God wants us to

> **If an association with fellow human beings such as spouses, friends, teachers, students, leaders and followers can impact one's life, will not an association with God impact our lives so much more?**

pray. He wants us to communicate with Him out of our own free will in order for Him to impart His nature into us to enable us to live victorious Christian lives. The influence of the world around us is so great, the trials we go through, the temptations we face, what we hear, see and feel are capable of rendering us spiritually bankrupt. It is, therefore, vital that we develop a consistent prayer life so that we can overcome this influence with the strength and anointing which we receive from God during prayer.

Result of Prayerlessness

We can explain the result of prayerlessness by examining what the outcomes of the cases cited would be in the absence of communication. For instance, when there is no communication between husbands and wives, the relationship will become sour, will lead to a distrust of the partners involved and will eventually fall on the rocks. When there is no community involvement and togetherness, progress will be hindered and nothing can be achieved on a broader scale for the benefit of the community. In the absence of communication among friends, the bond, intimacy and trust will wane and eventually there will be a falling apart of the relationship. When a teacher does not communicate with his students, there will be no transfer of information and the students will be lacking in knowledge. If leaders distance themselves from their followers, there will be no direction which will result in chaos and anarchy. "Where there is no vision, the people perish" (Proverbs 29:18a).

From the foregoing, it is obvious that lack of communication leads to disagreement, separation, confusion, breakdown of relationships, disunity and other consequences. In the same manner, lack of communication with God will lead to separation, disagreement, disunity, lack of direction, powerlessness, loss of anointing, lack of wisdom and other outcomes which will affect us adversely.

Prayerlessness in Schools

We are all witnesses of the effect of a lack of prayer in the school system. It is obvious that anything without God is bound to fail because He is the source of everything. Jesus said, "apart from me ye can do nothing" (John 15:5). The Bible says "The fear of the Lord is a foundation of life..." (Proverbs 14:27a). The devil fears prayer, fasting, the Word of God and the blood of Jesus. As said by Derek Prince, the devil will make every effort to prevent prayer in schools and every place. We are all reaping the fruits of a lack of prayer in schools. Some children have no regard for authority, for the elderly and for each other. The spirit of disobedience has taken the minds of some captive and they are pursuing after evil continually. Lying, sex, fighting, gangsterism, wickedness and the likes have become the way of life for many of them.

The current spate of crime is a direct result of this culture of prayerlessness and only heaven knows what the future holds for us all. The truth is God is the builder of the "house." If the Lord does not build the house, the builders will labor in vain. We should allow God to build the school system and the children without which all efforts will lead to futility. I believe that all is not lost. Christians should rise up and pray that God will bring back prayer into the schools for the sake of our children. II Chronicles 7:14 says, "if my people, who are called by my name, will humble themselves and pray and seek my face and turn from their wicked ways, then will I hear from heaven and will forgive their sin and will heal their land" (NIV). It is only through prayer that God can impact the lives of the young. In the absence of prayer we will lean on our own understanding, on the arm of flesh and are bound to be failures both in the spirit and in the natural.

Chapter 13

Newton's Law of Gravity Explains the Mystery of Prayer

*O*ur Lord Jesus Christ spoke and taught many times using parables as a tool of communicating His message to His followers. His parables are earthly stories that were used to explain spiritual or heavenly truths. Furthermore, parables are earthly, natural or scientific phenomenon that were used to explain spiritual truths. For example, the story of the prodigal son is an earthly story which explains God's forgiveness and acceptance of His people who backslide or sin against Him and return in repentance. The parable of the sower is another good example explaining the reasons why we respond to the Word of God in different ways.

Newton's Law of Universal Gravitation states that: The force of attraction between any two objects depends upon their masses and the distance between them. The further away an object moves from the center of gravity of the earth the less the force of gravity or the less attraction the earth has on the object. This explains why astronauts experience weightlessness and float in the atmosphere as they fly far into outer space away from the earth's gravitational pull.

This earthly or scientific phenomenon as explained by Isaac Newton can be used to further unlock the mystery of prayer. When we pray consistently without ceasing, we develop a strong relationship with God Almighty which results in a bond or intimacy between us and God. The closer we get to God through prayer, fasting and study of His Word, the more we experience the presence, the anointing and the power of God. A force of attraction develops between us and God. We get closer and closer to God and a time comes when we become one with God so that we tend to get absorbed into God. James 4:8a says, "Draw nigh to God, and he will draw nigh to you." The Apostle Paul got to this point in his walk with the Lord and became absorbed into God so much that he declared: "I am crucified with Christ: nevertheless I live; yet not I, but Christ liveth in me: and the life which I now live in the flesh I live by the faith of the Son of God, who loved me, and gave himself for me" (Galatians 2:20).

Jesus was one with God by His commitment to prayer and He declared, "I and my Father are one" (John 10:30). He also said, "Believest thou not that I am in the Father, and the Father in me? the words that I speak unto you I speak not of myself: but the Father that dwelleth in me, he doeth the works" (John 14:10).

When we do not pray or commune with God, we become like the astronauts who drift away from the earth's gravitation, float in outer space and no longer experience the attraction of the Earth's gravitational pull. In the spirit, we tend to drift away from God and begin to float. We are blown away by the wind of the enemy in any direction, he can bring fear, discouragement, hopelessness, loss of joy; we become vulnerable to any of his weapons and he can do anything to our lives at any time he chooses because we are far away from the presence, protection and attraction of God. Under such circumstances, we can easily be blown away by every wind of doctrine (Ephesians 4:14).

From another perspective, objects are much heavier when they are closer to the earth's center of gravity but experience weightlessness when they move further away from the earth's gravitational pull. The closer we get to God in prayer, the heavier we become with the anointing of God. The further away we get from God through prayerlessness, the less the anointing of God abides on us, and we become weightless in the Spirit. Nebuchadnezzar did not have a relationship with the God of Israel. He was far away from God. The Word of God came to him saying, "...Mene, Mene, Tekel, Upharsin. This is the interpretation of the thing: Mene; God hath numbered thy kingdom, and finished it. Tekel; Thou art weighed in the balances, and art found wanting" (Daniel 5:25b-27). He was weightless because he did not have the Spirit of God or anointing and God's presence was more or less absent from his life. He was blown away by the wind of the enemy and was turned into a monster.

Tying It All Up

When we pray, God talks back to us out of the abundance of His heart. His Word is spirit, has life and is backed with creativity and anointing which breaks yokes in our lives and gives us a breakthrough. These Words create faith, fruits and gifts of the Spirit which enable us to overcome sin and the devil and cause us to live Godly and victorious Christian lives and also do the miraculous (Acts 3:1-10). When communication continues, a time comes when we begin to agree with God. We become united with Him in thought, deed, power and anointing resulting in healing, deliverance and liberty; the nature of God is more or less transferred into our lives.

Reflecting on all the cases discussed and what transpires as a result of communication, we observe that marriage produces agreement; community involvement results in strength, power and authority; and friendship results in union, bonding and intimacy. Also, leaders wield an influential power which affects the perceptions and, therefore, the decisions of their followers and teachers transfer their thoughts to their students.

Christians are the bride of Christ, members of the body of Christ, friends of Christ and Jesus is our leader and teacher. We will, therefore, be in agreement, have strength, power and authority, be in union, have a bond of friendship and intimacy with Him. Our perceptions and decisions will be influenced by God and Christ's thoughts and knowledge will be transferred to us as we pray or communicate with God through our Master and Savior Christ Jesus the Lord.

As mentioned earlier, God wants to build a relationship with us through communication as Adam and Eve first had with Him. By so doing we become one with God and He comes to our aid when we need help, remembering that prayer is a relationship building with God just as we build relationships with our fellow man. What we receive in this relationship makes us victorious, successful and blessed both in the spirit and in the natural.

> **Prayer is a relationship building with God just as we build relationships with our fellow man.**

Raymond Finch writing on prayer said, "Like any relationship, it goes through stages, from acquaintance to friendliness, then on to friendship, love and finally union."

Levels of Communication

The outcome of communication depends on the level at which the parties involved are communicating. At this juncture I wish to emphasize that there are three levels at which communication can take place namely:

a) Positive to Positive

b) Positive to Negative

c) Negative to Negative

In the eleventh chapter of the book of Genesis, the sixth verse, God speaking of the people of Shinar said; "As one people speaking the same language..." (NIV). The observations that God made about these people connotes that there was understanding, love, unity, respect, focus and they had the same goal and that was to build the tower. They were positive and they could certainly achieve their goal or accomplish whatever they intended to do.

On one of my book signing tours, as I explained the effect of communication, one gentleman told me of how he had communicated with his wife but to no avail and that they were on the verge of divorce. I want to emphasize again at this point that communication may not necessarily yield positive results in all circumstances because if one party is communicating positively and the other party is communicating negatively, the outcome may not be positive.

What I mean by positive and negative is that if you are communicating out of love and your spouse is communicating out of anger and hate (probably because your spouse has made up his or her mind about another woman or man to whom he or she is talking), no good thing can come out of your communication. The outcome will depend on which of the two sides is "stronger."

When two parties are communicating with negative undertones there is no way that it could yield positive results. On the other hand, if both parties are communicating positively, which means in love, respect, unity and understanding with a common goal, the outcome will definitely be positive and they will both enjoy the positive outcomes of their communication such as love, unity, agreement and accomplishment as we find in the people of Shinar.

PART FOUR
Dynamics of Prayer

Chapter 14

Dynamics of Prayer

*P*rayer is fundamental to a successful Christian living because it helps us to have an intimate relationship with God, and without it there is no other way we can live Godly lives. Prayer does not have to be ritualistic, and as it does happen in any relationship between two individuals like a husband and wife, we should learn to "converse" with God. Father Tilden Edwards said about prayer, "Practice talking to God conversationally, in your own words, as a prelude to deeper, contemplative prayer. Relying totally on ritualistic prayer can be a way of evading God in the name of God."

Now that we know what goes on during prayer, we have a better understanding of what prayer is and what it does in the life of the one who practices it. We will examine some verses in the Bible which will reveal when, where and how prayer is supposed to be done effectively.

When to Pray

God has not given us any clear command as to when we should pray, however, we have some clues from Scripture. My wife, Gloria, once said, "One of the greatest

> **One of the greatest privileges of the child of God is that he does not have to make an appointment to go before God in prayer.**

privileges of the child of God is that he does not have to make an appointment to go before God in prayer." He is always available. He has no vacation time. He neither slumbers nor sleeps. He is a very present help in the time of need. He is working twenty-four hours a day, seven days a week and three hundred and sixty-five days a year.

We are admonished by Paul, the apostle, to pray without ceasing. He wrote in I Thessalonians 5:17, "pray continually" (NIV). From this verse we do know that there is no specific time that we ought to pray. Prayer can be done at anytime - in the morning, afternoon, evening or night. King David said "In the morning, O Lord, you hear my voice; in the morning I lay my requests before you and wait in expectation" (Psalm 5:3 NIV). "Evening, morning and noon I cry out in distress, and he hears my voice" (Psalm 55:17 NIV). Jesus prayed all night (Luke 6:12). In Acts 3:1 it is recorded, "Now Peter and John went up together into the temple at the hour of prayer, being the ninth hour." From this verse we also learn that we can have a set time devoted to prayer.

The body survives on food. Prayer and the Word are the food of the Spirit. We have to maintain a constant link with God through prayer and the study of His Word in order to keep our spirits alive and strong. We should, however, remember that we have to make a determined, planned, organized and disciplined effort to pray because it is the most important thing for us in our walk with the Lord.

Where to Pray

Prayers can be done anywhere since God is omnipresent. He is everywhere at the same time and can be called upon at any place. For example, from inside the belly of a fish, Jonah prayed to the Lord his God. He said: "In my distress I called to the Lord, and he answered me. From the depths of the grave, I called for help, and you listened to my cry" (Jonah 2:2 NIV). God heard Jonah's prayer from the belly of a fish in the depths of the sea. Jesus sometimes went to the mountainside to pray (Luke 6:12). Daniel also prayed in his room; "Now when Daniel learned that the decree had been published, he went home to his upstairs room where the windows opened toward Jerusalem. Three times a day he got down on his knees and prayed, giving thanks to his God, just as he had done before" (Daniel 6:10 NIV).

God hears our prayers when we call upon Him in our closets, on the highways, in the air, on the sea or in the temple; wherever we are, God will hear us. We have to understand, however, that prayer must be conducted in a quiet place in order for us to be able to focus on the communication with our Father without distractions. Jesus often times went to isolated and quiet places for prayer (Matthew 14:23).

Postures in Prayer

There is no rule in the Bible regarding a particular posture that should be used when we pray. For example, Jesus told His disciples, "And when you stand praying, if you hold anything against anyone, forgive him, so that your Father in heaven may forgive you your sins" (Mark 11:25 NIV). Jesus told the disciples that they could stand before God and pray to Him.

In Luke 22:41, it is said about Jesus that, "He withdrew about a stone's throw beyond them, knelt down and prayed" (NIV). Jesus sometimes prayed while kneeling down and other times He fell on His face, but He did not make these postures a rule. In Matthew 26:39a it is written, "Going a little farther, He fell with his face to the ground and prayed" (NIV).

In Acts 21:5 the apostle Paul recorded, "But when our

time was up, we left and continued on our way. All the disciples and their wives and children accompanied us out of the city, and there on the beach we knelt to pray" (NIV).

The prophet Elisha walked back and forth (paced up and down) in his guest room while praying for God's intervention in the death of the Shunamite woman's son (II Kings 4:35). Our postures in prayer will depend much on how the Spirit of God leads us or that which we find convenient depending on the circumstances.

Individual and Corporate Prayer

Prayers can be done individually or corporately. Matthew 14:23 says about Jesus, "After he had dismissed them, he went up on a mountainside by himself to pray. When evening came, he was there alone" (NIV).

It is of utmost importance that every individual should develop a personal relationship with the Lord. Every parent should teach and encourage their children to have a personal quality time with God in order to know God for themselves. Proverbs 22:6 says, "Train up a child in the way he should go: and when he is old, he will not depart from it." Knowledge of God can neither be transferred to anyone nor can it be inherited from parents. Each and every individual is responsible for their own relationship with the Lord and for their spiritual development. Kathryn Kuhlman said, "The greatest power that God has given to any individual is the power of prayer," as quoted by Benny Hinn.

Matthew 18:20 says, "Where two or three are gathered together in my name, there am I in the midst of them." In Acts 12:12 we are told about Peter that, "When this had dawned on him, he went to the house of Mary the mother of John, also called

Mark, where many people had gathered and were praying" (NIV). The disciples assembled on the day of Pentecost and waited for the promise of the Holy Ghost as Jesus had told them (Acts 2:1). There is no limit to the number of people that can offer prayers to God as is revealed in the verses above. The Bible says in Deuteronomy 32:30, one shall chase a thousand and two shall chase ten thousand. Sometimes there may be a need to seek the support of other trusted brethren to pray on some issues because of the power of corporate prayer. Matthew 18:20 says, if two shall agree on earth as touching anything that they shall ask, it shall be done unto them of my father which is in heaven.

Time Constraints in Prayer

Many people find it difficult to spend time with God. They tend to run short of words after a few minutes in prayer. Looking at the example of Jesus and the apostles we realize that there are no time constraints on prayer, but in order to build a healthy relationship with God we have to spend time with Him. If God is everything to us, then we should be able to develop a meaningful relationship where we do have time for Him and with Him.

In the natural we cannot develop any relationships with people with whom we only exchange greetings. We only start developing a relationship when we pause and relate through communication. Jesus sometimes spent all night praying (Luke 6:12). He told his disciples, you could not spend even one hour (Matthew 26:40). "Even one hour" presupposes that an hour could possibly be the minimum amount of time to spend in prayer. It is

> **In the natural we cannot develop any relationships with people with whom we only exchange greetings. We only start developing a relationship when we pause and relate through communication.**

the desire of any loving parent to spend time with the family in order to build strong and healthy relationships. The same applies to God because we are His children.

Some people are in the habit of praying for about five minutes each day. In the natural, what kind of relationship can we develop with our spouses or other relations if we only spend five minutes a day in communication. As it is in the natural, so it is in the spiritual. We cannot develop any meaningful or healthy relationship with God if we pray for only five minutes every day. After studying the types of prayer, you would begin to realize that praying for one hour could be a normal experience and that no amount of time would be too much to spend before God. As you develop a relationship with God, you would come to know that God's presence is the sweetest place one could ever be. The Psalmist said, "In thy presence is fullness of joy; at thy right hand there are pleasures for evermore" (Psalm 16:11b).

If we really "go" before the Lord in prayer, we come from His presence knowing that our sins are forgiven, our strength is renewed, our prayers are answered and that the presence of the Lord will be with us as we go about our daily activities. We will be able to accomplish more on the job, school, etc. when we are prayed up rather than relegating prayer.

Praying in the Name of Jesus

The name of Jesus Christ is exalted above every other name. In His name we have salvation, deliverance and our victory. Acts 4:12 says, "Salvation is found in no one else, for there is no other name under heaven given to men by which we must be saved" (NIV). In John 14:6, Jesus made a claim that is unparalleled. He said, "I am the way, the truth, and the life: no man cometh unto the Father, but by me." It takes someone who is more than a man to make such a claim. He did not say that He is one of the ways to get to the Father. He is the "Only Way." The following Scriptural verses support the claim of Jesus.

Jesus declared, "I and my Father are one" (John 10:30). "Before Abraham was, I am" (John 8:58b). When Philip asked Jesus to show them the Father, Jesus answered by saying, I have been long with you and you ask me to show you the father. Don't you know that if you see me then you have seen the father? (John 14:8,9). The testimony of the Lord Jesus Christ is unsurpassed. There is no one that has ever been able to make such claims and support them with signs and wonders and there will never be. He healed the sick, raised the dead, cast out demons, the wind and the sea obeyed Him, He died, was buried and He rose from the dead. He is alive forever more and worthy to be praised.

Philippians 2:9-11 says, "Therefore God exalted him to the highest place and gave him the name that is above every name, that at the name of Jesus every knee should bow, in heaven and on earth and under the earth, and every tongue confess that Jesus Christ is Lord, to the glory of God the Father" (NIV). At the mention of the name of Jesus, Satan and his demons tremble. In Ephesians 4:8-10 the Apostle Paul wrote, "This is why it says: 'When he ascended on high, he led captives in his train and gave gifts to men.' (What does 'he ascended' mean except that he also descended to the lower, earthly regions? He who descended is the very one who ascended higher than all the heavens, in order to fill the whole universe.)" (NIV).

Jesus Christ fills the whole universe. He fills heaven, the earth and He fills the lower earthly regions. He is All In All, and He is Omnipresent. He is Lord, and He alone qualifies to be worshipped. Jesus is the only one who lived and was tempted in all points and was yet without sin. This feat shows the uniqueness of Jesus Christ. At His baptism it is written that a voice came from heaven and declared, "You are my Son, whom

I love; with you I am well pleased" (Mark 1:11 NIV). God is a spirit and we are made of spirit, soul and body. It takes someone who had the nature of God, lived with Him and knows Him to be qualified to show us who God is, and that person is Jesus Christ our Lord because He was a spirit from the beginning, lived with God before His manifestation in the flesh.

> **It takes someone who had the nature of God, lived with Him and knows Him to be qualified to show us who God is.**

Jesus alone knows God because He had the nature of God and lived with Him before He was manifested to live among us. John 1:18 says, "No man hath seen God at any time; the only begotten Son, which is in the bosom of the Father, he hath declared him." Matthew 11:27 also says, "...No one knows the Son except the Father, and no one knows the Father except the Son and those to whom the Son chooses to reveal him" (NIV). In the natural no one can help us to know somebody with whom they have never come into contact or have never known. Jesus is the only one who had the "physical" contact with God. They were together at the creation. Genesis 1:26a says, "And God said, Let us make man in our image, after our likeness."

Colossians 1:15-17 says, "Who is the image of the invisible God, the firstborn of every creature: For by him were all things created, that are in heaven, and that are in earth, visible and invisible, whether they be thrones, or dominions, or principalities, or powers: all things were created by him, and for him: And he is before all things, and by him all things consist."

Jesus is Lord indeed and we can ask anything in His name and He will do it according to His promise in John 14:13: "And whatsoever ye shall ask in my name, that will I do, that the Father may be glorified in the Son." At the crucifixion of Jesus, the criminal who had repented of his sin was given the full right by Jesus to enter into paradise. In Luke 23:43b Jesus proclaimed, "Today you will be with me in paradise" (NIV). Sometimes I wonder why some people reject the love and mercy of Christ. The fact that Jesus is God is an undeniable and unquestionable truth. His words prove it. His works prove it. His life, death, burial and resurrection all prove and bear witness that Jesus is Lord, and He is the Savior of the world. Hallelujah!

Praying Scripturally

The Word of God is His will for our lives; therefore, when our prayer is based on the Word of God, we put Him in remembrance of what He has promised concerning us. The Lord said, "Put me in remembrance: let us plead together: declare thou, that thou mayest be justified" (Isaiah 43:26). Jeremiah 29:11 says, "For I know the thoughts that I think toward you, saith the Lord...." When our prayers are Scriptural, God is bound by His Word to perform what He has promised because "God is not a man, that he should lie; neither the son of man, that he should repent: hath he said, and shall he not do it?" (Numbers 23:19). Let us put Him in remembrance of His will for us for He is faithful to do what He has promised.

The Three Petitions

The story is told of three women who went to God with their petitions. The first of the three women was married to a man for many years. They had children together and fortunately, the man had the privilege of traveling to another country for greener pastures. For a very long time he did not come home although he kept in touch with his family. Unfortunately, this man fell in love with another woman and got married to her.

As time elapsed, the relationship with the second wife grew cold and sour; the man started staying out because he had found another woman. The first woman was fasting and praying for God to bring her husband back to her. The second woman also started fasting and praying aggressively for her husband to have a change of heart so he would come back. The third woman was praying and thanking God for bringing her a man who would be her future husband. She would always thank, praise and worship God for answering her prayer. Here are three strong petitions all directed to God. What should God do? You be the best judge. The revelation here is that many times we fast and pray amiss because our prayer has no scriptural basis. The second woman did not consider the fact that the man was married before she met him and that she was an adulterer. The third woman did not wait to question the fact that the man had a long history of relationships. The first woman is the rightful wife of the man. We should pray according to God's will and His Word.

Praying in Faith

In Hebrews 10:22 the writer admonishes us to come before God with a sincere heart in full assurance of faith without a divided attentiveness knowing that He is in a position to deliver us in our time of difficulty. He is faithful to do what we have committed to His hand against that day. God never flounders on His promises. The writer of the letter of James 1:6 says that we cannot receive any good thing from God without faith. Faith is, therefore, an important ingredient for receiving answers from God. Hebrews 11:2 says, "For by it the elders obtained a good report." We should develop our faith by hearing the Word of God, studying and fellowshipping with other believers.

We now have a clear understanding of how prayer works God's attributes into our lives. Faith is one of God's attributes which we gain as we commune with God. Romans 10:17 says,

"So then faith cometh by hearing, and hearing by the word of God." During prayer, God communicates to us and His Words produce or release faith in us. Fasting on the other hand sharpens and quickens our faith by sharpening and quickening our hearing capabilities which we will discuss in Part Eight.

Praying in the Spirit

When we enter God's presence in fervent prayer, the Holy Spirit assists us. Ephesians 6:18 talks about praying in the spirit in all our prayers. John 4:24 says, "God is spirit, and his worshippers must worship in spirit and in truth" (NIV). In this context "in spirit" means worshipping God in sincerity of heart, in genuineness, honesty and without deceit. In the same way, praying in the Spirit in the context of the sixth chapter of Ephesians refers to sharing genuine, honest feelings in our supplication with our Maker in sincerity of heart with fervency and without deceit. It also means pouring out one's heart to the Lord. Jesus' prayer in the Garden of Gethsemane is a typical example of pouring out one's heart. Luke 22:44 says that Jesus prayed earnestly and His sweat was like drops of blood.

In the letter of Paul to the Romans 8:26, 27, he wrote, "In the same way, the Spirit helps us in our weakness. We do not know what we ought to pray for, but the Spirit himself intercedes for us with groans that words cannot express. And he who searches our hearts knows the mind of the Spirit, because the Spirit intercedes for the saints in accordance with God's will" (NIV). When one receives the baptism of the Holy Spirit, he or she may pray in an unknown tongue as the Holy Spirit Himself gives utterance because Acts 2:4 says, "And they were all filled with the Holy Ghost, and began to speak with other tongues, as the Spirit gave them utterance." Sometimes when we do not know how to pray effectively, the Holy Spirit Himself intercedes on our behalf.

115

NOTES:

PART FIVE
Types of Prayer

Chapter 15

Types of Prayer

As I journeyed with a friend and shared this revelation on unlocking the mystery of prayer, he questioned that our communication with God is different from our communication with our fellow man. That sounded very reasonable to me, so I thought it over for a moment. Then I thought of Genesis 1:26a where it is written, "And God said, Let us make man in our image, after our likeness." The fact that we are able to communicate with our fellow man is an attribute of God, because He created us in His likeness. God created us for this purpose, so that we may have fellowship with Him and with one another through communication.

Our communication with God is not different from our communication with our fellow man. The only difference is that God is a spirit, and we are spirit and flesh. God, therefore, communicates to our spirits through various means and He uses human vessels to communicate to our flesh. We shall dwell more on this topic under the title "How Does God Talk Back to Us?"

Jesus taught us how to pray by teaching the Lord's Prayer in Matthew 6:9-13. In Ephesians 6:18a, Paul also admonished the believers to pray with all prayers in the Spirit. There are different types of prayers as is embodied in the Lord's Prayer which is more or less a model prayer. There we find prayers of thanksgiving, praise, worship, supplications, confessions, intercessions and warfare. The type of prayer we offer depends on our relationship with God and the circumstances in which we find ourselves.

Prayer of Meditation

An Act of Spiritual Evaluation

After the death of Moses, God told Joshua, "Only be thou strong and very courageous, that thou mayest observe to do according to all the law, which Moses my servant commanded thee: turn not from it to the right hand or to the left, that thou mayest prosper whithersoever thou goest. This book of the law shall not depart out of thy mouth; but thou shalt meditate therein day and night, that thou mayest observe to do according to all that is written therein: for then thou shalt make thy way prosperous, and then thou shalt have good success" (Joshua 1:7-8).

God demanded observation and obedience to His Word as a prerequisite for prosperity and good success. We examine ourselves during meditation to see if we are in the will of God or in the faith. Let every man examine himself whether he is in the faith (II Corinthians 13:5a). The Word of God is our standard for righteousness.

As we meditate, the Word of God becomes a "mirror" or a "microscope" through which we search ourselves to see if we are reflecting His will, walking in obedience or if there is any sin in our lives. If we do not see ourselves in the will of God, then we have the opportunity to make the necessary confessions and amendments to be able to live up to God's expectations. Paul writing to Timothy revealed that: "All scripture is given by inspiration of God, and is profitable for doctrine, for reproof, for correction, for instruction in righteousness: That the man of God may be perfect, thoroughly furnished unto all good works" (II Timothy 3:16,17). The Word of God rebukes and corrects us of any unrighteousness in our lives. The Psalmist declares that the Word of God is a light to our path and a lamp to our feet (Psalm 119:105). Let us reflect on some of the functions of light: it helps us to see our way out of darkness, it prevents us from falling into pits and ditches and it helps to give us direction and guidance. Therefore, if we meditate on the Word of God, it will keep us from sin, and we will be able to walk uprightly. It will save us from evil and also give us direction and guidance.

The Psalmist declared, "Blessed is the man that walketh not in the counsel of the ungodly, nor standeth in the way of sinners, nor sitteth in the seat of the scornful. But his delight is in the law of the Lord; and in his law doth he meditate day and night" (Psalm 1:1-2). Meditation on the Word of God is a necessary prerequisite for prosperity according to the writers of the books of Joshua and the Psalms.

Dick Eastman wrote, "Meditation is more than merely thinking good thoughts. It is the giving of attention to how we might specifically apply these ponderings after the devotional hour has ended."

An Act of Spiritual Reflection

The Psalmist declares in Psalm 8:3,4: "When I consider your heavens, the work of your fingers, the moon and the stars, which you have set in place, what is man that you are mindful of him, the son of man that you care for him?" (NIV). Meditation helps to reflect on the goodness of God to us in the past and on His greatness which leads us to thank, praise and worship Him.

Revelations 12:11a says, "And they overcame him by the blood of the Lamb, and by the word of their testimony..." Our testimonies of past victories strengthen our faith and give us the confidence to put our requests before the Lord. King David remembered his testimony when the Israelites were being mocked by Goliath and the Philistines. He reflected on how God had delivered him from lions and bears when he was shepherding his father's flock. He remembered how God had given him strength to overpower the lion and bear to deliver the lambs from their paws. He said, my God is able to deliver this uncircumcised Philistine into my hands, therefore, he had the courage to confront Goliath and defeated him in the name of the Lord (I Samuel 17:36).

Chapter 16

Prayer of Thanksgiving

An Act of Appreciation

We thank others for things done for us or for someone else. In the same manner we need to thank God in order to show our appreciation for the many blessings He has showered upon us such as forgiveness of our sins, our salvation, healing of our diseases, provision of jobs, spouse, children, food, clothing, shelter and His love toward us or others. We have to thank Him for His mercy, kindness, faithfulness, tolerance, compassion and trustworthiness. The songwriter composed, "Count your many blessings and name them one by one and it will surprise you what the Lord has done." There are countless blessings that the Lord has bestowed on us both spiritually and naturally of which we tend to be unaware.

When we thank the Lord, we show our appreciation and gratitude to Him and when He sees gratitude in us, it pleases God and it opens the door for Him to shower more of His blessings on us. God delights in our being thoughtful of His goodness.

God's Will for Us

I Thessalonians 5:18 says, "In every thing give thanks: for this is the will of God in Christ Jesus concerning you." I believe that almost every one might have asked this question at some time, "How could it ever be the will of a loving Father for

His children to go through suffering and pain and thank Him in it? God did not say that we should thank Him in some situations or only when we are strong or blessed in one way or the other, but in all things He said we should give thanks. In sickness, sorrow, tears, joblessness and no matter how devastating the circumstance may be we should always give thanks in all things. Even in death situations we should give thanks.   (More will follow on this subject under "Does God Answer Prayer?" Chapter 24)

Looking back at the testimony, praise and character that is produced as a result of suffering will help us to understand the workings of God. The late Rev. Kenneth Hagin Jr. was sick to the point of death before he experienced the saving power and deliverance of God. Through this experience and testimony, Kenneth Hagin has been used mightily of God to touch the hearts of millions around the world.

Rev. Oral Roberts was sick with tuberculosis almost to the point of death when he was healed miraculously by God. We all can bear testimony of how he has been mightily used of God to bring deliverance to multitudes. I Corinthians 10:13 says, "There hath no temptation taken you but such as is common to man: but God is faithful, who will not suffer you to be tempted above that ye are able; but will with the temptation also make a way to escape, that ye may be able to bear it." If we are able to thank God in our sufferings, it reveals the level of our faith in God's Word and the trust we have in Him, that He is Almighty, All Sufficient, He is in control and has a better plan for our lives and that He will make everything work together for our good even in unfavorable circumstances.

An Act of Obedience

In 2 Timothy 3:16-17, the Apostle Paul tells us that the Word of God "…is given by inspiration of God, and is profitable for doctrine, for reproof, for correction, for instruction in righteousness: That the man of God may be perfect, thoroughly furnished unto all good works." We have to obey Scripture in its entirety because it is the Word of God, and as believers it is for our training in righteousness because of the benefits that we derive from obeying God's Word. We obey God when we thank and appreciate Him in all circumstances.

Ingratitude Hurts Badly

On many occasions we have all been hypocrites. We have complained about people who have not shown any sign of gratitude when we felt that we have been kind to them. While we are complaining, the phone rings or there is a knock on the door. There comes the one we have been thinking about. The caller comes with a word of appreciation or a card to say thank you. Then we respond, "Oh, you did not have to bother yourself, or there was no need for you to go through all that. It was just a token of my love to you." These actions are natural instincts or actions which tell how important it is for us to show gratitude to people who have been kind or have loved us because good people are sometimes hard to find.

Ingratitude can cut deeply into the heart and cause wounds. It is a very "bitter pill" to swallow. We should always remember that God created us in His image and likeness and He feels the same way that we do in many situations. In the natural, which of us would want to do anything for a person who is ungrateful and unappreciative of anything we do for them? "And Jesus answering said, Were there not ten cleansed? but where are the nine? There are not found that returned to give glory to God, save this stranger. And he said unto him, Arise, go thy way: thy faith hath made thee whole" (Luke 17:17-19).

Sometimes I marvel at Jesus' comment about the unthankful lepers who were cleansed because He has the natural ability to provide everything we need. In spite of this fact, Jesus still expected appreciation from them. I am inclined to believe that He said this to remind us of the danger of being unthankful, which I believe can hinder us from receiving blessings in the future.

An Act of Faith

In the natural, if we approach someone for help or any kind of assistance and the person responds positively all the time, there comes a time when we will instinctively thank the person if he promised to do something for us on particular date although we do not have a physical evidence of the promise. We thank the person because we are confident that he will not fail us because he has always been faithful to his word in the past and has always been there for us.

In the same way, there are countless things that God has done and is still doing and His promises are many for us; therefore, thanking God is a demonstration of a very high level of faith. If we thank the Lord for prayers not yet answered with an anticipation of receiving the answer, there is no room left for doubt. Like praise, it shows the confidence and trust we have in God. Jesus applied this principle when he brought Lazarus back to life. The Word of God declares, "So they took away the

> **If we thank the Lord for prayers not yet answered with an anticipation of receiving the answer, there is no room left for doubt.**

stone. Then Jesus looked up and said 'Father, I thank you that you have heard me. I knew that you always hear me, but I said this for the benefit of the people standing here, that they may believe that you sent me'" (John 11:41, 42 NIV).

Lazarus' body was decomposing when Jesus arrived at the grave because he had been dead for four days. Jesus needed a high level of faith to restore the cells, tissues, organs and systems that were completely dismembered and in disarray. Decomposition had already set in but thanksgiving brought about the miracle.

I sought the Lord in prayer and fasting for two days every week for my deliverance from an infirmity. For a long time I did not get any breakthrough. One fateful day, after breaking my fast as usual, I knew too well that I had not made any progress. Then I heard an inner voice telling me to stop asking and rather thank God for my healing. I responded to the leading of the Spirit and to the glory of God I started feeling better and better from then on. I believe that God used the prayer of thanksgiving to remove any uncertainty or doubt in me that served as a hindrance to receiving my deliverance.

When Jesus arrived at Lazarus' tomb, He never screamed, He did not bind the spirit of death nor did He curse the spirit behind death. He simply gave thanks to God, and this brought about an unforgettable miracle in the history of Christianity.

An Act of Humility

When gratitude and appreciation flows from our hearts to the Lord, we are in a way telling God that He is the one who has made it possible for us to be successful or accomplish anything but not of our own strength or ability. When God sees humility in us, He will promote us; He will exalt us because the Bible says, Anyone who humbles himself shall be exalted and anyone who exalts himself shall be humbled.

This brings to mind the rich man who had said to his soul in the gospel of Luke 12:18-20, "And he said, This will I do: I will pull down my barns, and build greater; and there will I bestow all my fruits and my goods. And I will say to my soul, Soul, thou hast much goods laid up for many years; take thine ease, eat, drink, and be merry. But God said unto him, Thou fool, this night thy soul shall be required of thee: then whose shall those things be, which thou hast provided?" The rich man did not appreciate God for blessing the work of his hands. He attributed his success to his own ability instead of giving the glory to God.

Chapter 17

Prayer of Praise

*P*raise is defined as: "to commend the worth of, express approval or admiration or to laud the glory of God," according to Webster's New World College Dictionary. We praise people for their achievements, appearance or personal qualities. For example we praise our spouses, children or friends for their academic achievements or certain unique characteristics that they possess. In the same way, we praise God for His wisdom, power, beauty, holiness, righteous judgment and so on. God is to be praised even for His creation, that is, His handiwork, for His thoughtfulness and for what He has done. He created the heavens and the earth, the sea, all the plants and animals and gave us dominion over them.

The Psalmist declared, "I will extol the Lord at all times; his praise will always be on my lips. My soul will boast in the Lord; let the afflicted hear and rejoice. Glorify the Lord with me; let us exalt his name together" (Psalm 34:1-3 NIV). Moses and the children of Israel praised God when they were miraculously delivered from the Egyptian army. They sang:

"Thy right hand, O Lord, is become glorious in power: thy right hand, O Lord, hath dashed in pieces the enemy. And in the greatness of thine excellency thou hast overthrown them that rose up against thee: thou sentest forth thy wrath, which consumed them as stubble. And with the blast of thy nostrils the waters were gathered together, the floods stood upright as an heap, and the depths were congealed in the heart of the sea" (Exodus 15:6-8).

Results of Praise

One beautiful Sunday morning, as I was talking to a lady after our church service, her eyes fell on my shoes and she passed a comment, "Your shoes are very nice." I looked at my shoes and started developing the confidence that I had beautiful shoes on. From that moment onwards, after almost every two or three steps I took, I would look down at my shoes and admire them. How confident and happy I felt about that. I had worn the shoes for quite some time, but until the lady passed that praise remark, I had never felt that way before.

We know from the foregoing that praise brings realization or self-awareness, gladness and a sense of accomplishment and acceptance on the part of the person being praised. It makes the person feel appreciated, exalted and boosts one's confidence and, therefore, prides themselves in their achievements. If anyone praises you, it is most probable that you will end up thinking, "After all, I am not that bad." Praise, therefore, causes people to realize that they have potential and places them in a position to want to do better than before. For example, if you praise your child for a good report card, the child would want to do better the next time. This principle applies in all relationships and spheres of life such as with spouses, children, parents, employees, employer, students and friends. Praise releases and causes an explosion in

> **Praise releases and causes an explosion in all the potential of the person to perform to the best of his or her ability.**

all the potential of the person to perform to the best of his or her ability.

God has created us in His image and He also reacts to praise by giving of His best for us. Praising God also shows our absolute confidence and trust in Him. Praise exalts God to His rightful position and He begins to release His power to act on our behalf when He sees appreciation in us and also our confidence and trust in Him. This is the secret that causes God to shower His blessings upon us when we praise Him, for it is written that God inhabits the praise of His people (Psalm 22:3). When our praise goes up, His blessings come down. He is increased as we decrease.

This reminds me of when Paul and Silas were incarcerated. It is recorded that when they began to pray and sing praises unto God, suddenly there was a great earthquake and the foundations of the prison were shaken and immediately all the doors were open and every one's bonds were loosed (Acts 16:25,26). When they acknowledged the excellence of God's power and greatness, He felt the trust of the men in His authority and dominion. He was obligated to act on behalf of His people. God responds to the faith and trust of His people.

Victory Through Praise

During the reign of King Jehoshaphat, the Moabites, Ammonites and the people from Mount Seir came against the people of Judah in battle. The King feared greatly because the enemies were such a great multitude and he proclaimed a fast throughout all Judah and cried to God for help. The Lord heard their cry and promised they would not need to fight in the battle and that He was going to fight for them. King Jehoshaphat then appointed singers to the Lord that should praise God as they went out to battle. I believe they sang a song such as this:

You are the mighty man in battle, El Shaddai;
You are the mighty man in battle, Jehovah Nissi;
You are the mighty man in battle, El Shaddai;
You are the mighty man in battle, Glory to Your name!

When they began to sing and praise God, the Lord set ambushments against the children of Ammon, Moab, and Mount Seir and they fought against one another and smote themselves. King Jehoshaphat and the children of Israel returned with great spoil and joy.

The story of Judah's victory is recorded in II Chronicles 20:23,24 that, "The men of Ammon and Moab rose up against the men from Mount Seir to destroy and annihilate them. After they finished slaughtering the men from Seir, they helped to destroy one another. When the men of Judah came to the place that overlooks the desert and looked toward the vast army, they saw only dead bodies lying on the ground; no one had escaped" (NIV).

This victory shows how effective and powerful praise is. Sometimes God's approach to solving problems looks very simple, irrational and naïve, but I Corinthians 1:27 says, God uses the foolish things of this world to confound the wise, and in His plan and purpose is His wisdom and power. Through praise God proves His power, and mighty miracles and victories are won by His people. By praise the walls of Jericho also came tumbling down (Joshua 6:20). Let us begin to praise God in spite of walls of disease, failure, marital problems and all other kinds of mountains that confront us and see God fight on our behalf and bring them down like the walls of Jericho.

Chapter 18

Prayer of Worship

What is it About?

Worship and praise of God have been used and applied interchangeably. However, taking a second look at worship and praise reveals that they are two different prayer issues. We can praise people for certain achievements, and we can also praise God, but we cannot worship anybody except God.

The New International Webster's Pocket Dictionary gives a very clear definition of worship: "Worship is adoration, homage, rituals, prayers, etc. used in paying tribute to a deity." Therefore, we should draw a distinction between Praise and Worship. Worship has several connotations namely:

a) We worship God when we come together as a congregation of believers in a church service (Jeremiah 26:2).

b) When we offer praise, thanksgiving, supplication, offering, confession and all other activities that render service to God either individually in prayer or congregationally, we are worshipping God as the Almighty (Isaiah 66:23).

c) We also worship God in spirit and truth as we

live holy and righteous lives: that is allowing our minds and hearts to be controlled by the Spirit of God. "Therefore, I urge you, brothers, in view of God's mercy, to offer your bodies as living sacrifices, holy and pleasing to God - this is your spiritual act of worship" (Romans 12:1 NIV). "God is spirit, and his worshipers must worship in spirit and in truth" (John 4:24 NIV).

d) The type of worship I am talking about is the worship that can be ascribed to God and God only by the fruit of our lips for who He is (worship as defined in the Webster's dictionary).

We can praise people for their accomplishments (I Corinthians 11:2, II Corinthians 8:18) but I am talking about the accolade (praise) that can be ascribed to God only. That is worship, because He is unique, His ways are past finding out, He is Supreme, He is Wonderful, He is King of Kings and He is Lord of all. I believe this is the kind of worship that Jesus Christ prescribed for us in the Lord's Prayer. He taught us to hallow (reverence) the name of God (Luke 11:2).

Attributes of God

Let us ascribe to God the glory and honor that belongs to Him alone and no one else. He is the only one whose name can be hallowed. The following are some attributes that can be used to worship God:

- He is Elohim (the Creator)
- El Elyon (the God Most High)
- El Roi (the God who Sees)
- El Shaddai (the All Sufficient One)

134

- Adonai (The Lord)
- Jehovah (the Self-Existent One)
- Jehovah Jireh (the Lord our Provider)
- Jehovah Nissi (the Lord my Banner)
- Jehovah Mekoddishkem (the Lord who Sanctifies You)
- Jehovah Shalom (the Lord our Peace)
- Jehovah Sabaoth (the Lord of Hosts)
- Jehovah Raah (the Lord is my Shepherd)
- Jehovah Tsidkenu (the Lord our Righteousness)
- Jehovah Shammah (the Lord is There)
- Jehovah Rophi (the Lord our Healer)
- Omniscient (All Knowing)
- Omnipotent (All Powerful)
- Omnipresent (Present Everywhere)
- The Great I Am
- The Rock of Ages
- The God of Israel
- The God of Abraham
- The God of Isaac
- The God of Jacob
- King of Kings
- Lord of Lords
- The Lion of the Tribe of Judah
- Eternal King
- Immortal
- Invisible, the only wise God to be honored and glorified forever and ever!
- Everlasting Father, Sitting on the Throne of Majesty
- Glorious King
- Father of the Universe, Clothed in Heavenly Glory
- He is Wonderful, Amazing and Awesome
- Counselor

- Mighty God
- The Everlasting Father
- The Prince of Peace
- The Bright and Morning Star
- The Rose of Sharon
- The Lily of the Valley
- The Ancient of Days
- Immutable
- The Alpha and Omega (The First and the Last), Righteousness and Justice are the foundation of your throne, to your name be Glory, Honor, Power and Wisdom, Holy are you, Lord!

Listen to how King Hezekiah worshiped the Lord before he presented his petition in II Kings 19:15, "And Hezekiah prayed to the Lord: 'O Lord, God of Israel, enthroned between the cherubim, you alone are God over all the kingdoms of the earth'" (NIV). This is worship.

The Apostle Paul in ending the first chapter of his letter to Timothy, worshiped thus, "Now unto the King eternal, immortal, invisible, the only wise God, be honor and glory forever and ever. Amen!" (I Timothy 1:17).

Is there a living being, King, President, Prime Minister or Power that be to whom we can ascribe any of the above attributes? The Bible says that God is a jealous God and He will not share His glory with any man or idols (Exodus 34:14). Let us, therefore, worship God with attributes that cannot be ascribed to anyone else but God.

Jesus is Lord

Jesus Christ accepted worship from Thomas because He was God incarnate (John 20:28). He also declared, "Before

Abraham was, I am" (John 8:58). "I and my Father are one" (John 10:30). I have heard that Jesus is Lord, I have read that He is Lord and I have seen Him in a dream appearing in the clouds. He was so mighty that I could not look upon Him. He was majestic. I shivered and trembled in His presence, and then He vanished into the clouds. I have experienced Him; I have felt His presence. He is Lord and His Word is true. He is coming back in the same manner that He went up (Acts 1:11). It is certain. It will not fail. It will not falter, and it shall come to pass. We will have no choice but to bow down and worship Him, and no one can deny Him because He is coming back as the Lord.

> "For to us a child is born, to us a son is given, and the government will be on his shoulders. And he will be called Wonderful Counselor, Mighty God, Everlasting Father, Prince of Peace. Of the increase of his government and peace there will be no end. He will reign on David's throne and over his kingdom, establishing and upholding it with justice and righteousness from that time on and forever. The zeal of the Lord Almighty will accomplish this" (Isaiah 9:6, 7 NIV).

Results of Worship

Worship is an invitation to God to take control as the Supreme Lord of all. As we worship God, He is exalted in our hearts. He increases and we decrease; we begin to feel His presence, then His power and anointing comes over us and works through us. The anointing has many benefits:

a) Breaks the yoke of bondage and empowers us to heal the sick, cast out demons and to do the works of God (Isaiah 10:27).

b) Teaches us and causes us to understand the

Word of God in order to know more about Him
(1 John 2:27).

In conclusion, worship is acknowledgement that God
alone is God and He alone is All in All and the Supreme Lord of
All.

Chapter 19

Prayer of Confession

Sin is a Spirit

God created the world with the words of His mouth and according to Jesus, words are spirits and they give life. This is found in John 6:63 where Jesus said, "The words that I speak unto you, they are spirit, and they are life." It is therefore logical to conclude that words such as envy, anger and the act of stealing are spirits and they destroy life. Due to the inherent power that words possess, one good word can encourage and lift us up and in the same way an evil word can discourage and dampen our spirits because words are spirits.

When we confess or speak out our sins to God or our fellowman as the Bible admonishes us to do, God forgives us and the evil spirit behind the sin departs from us, and we experience our liberty. Romans 10:10 says, "For with the heart man believeth unto righteousness; and with the mouth confession is made unto salvation." When sin is not confessed, it remains with us and causes much damage in us because it is an evil spirit. This is the reason why we tend to lose our peace and joy and become frustrated and confused until we confess our sins.

Transparency

King David knew the secret of confession and in spite of his adultery with Bathsheba and murder of her husband Uriah,

God called him a man after His own heart. David lived a life of transparency before God because he confessed his sins instantly when he realized sin in his life. I call it "David's Principle." The prophet Nathan told David; A certain rich man had many sheep and cattle and a poor man had only one ewe lamb. The rich man had guests and instead of slaughtering one of his sheep, he went and took the ewe belonging to the poor man and slaughtered it for his guest (II Samuel 12:1-7). King David replied, this man deserves to die. Then the prophet told him, you are the one. "Then David said to Nathan, 'I have sinned against the Lord.' Nathan replied, 'The Lord has taken away your sin. You are not going to die'" (II Samuel 12:13 NIV).

The prophet Nathan pronounced many curses upon David and his house as a result of his evil deeds, but when David repented and confessed his sins, God forgave him and removed the curses. We see here, the power of confession in demonstration. God understands our tendency to err or do wrong sometimes and, therefore, it is how we handle our sins that matters most to God. David did not try to cover his sins, he did not try to be smart with God, and he did not blame someone else for his sins but repented instantly and confessed.

> **God understands our tendency to err or do wrong sometimes and, therefore, it is how we handle our sins that matters most to God.**

Since the Garden of Eden, people do not want to accept their faults. Adam blamed Eve, and Eve shifted blame on the serpent. Men do not want to be condemned for anything. We are only interested in the praise of men. We always want to justify our actions, shift blame and give excuses for our wrong doings and sometimes we use Scripture to defend ourselves. Looking back at the life of David and Paul, I have identified one of the secrets of their greatness and that is they accepted their faults, repented and made confessions. In I Timothy 1:15b Paul declared, "This is a faithful saying, and worthy of all acceptation, that Christ Jesus came into the world to save sinners; of whom I am chief." Paul was not shy of confessing, neither was he proud. He made an open confession as an example to believers. In the gospel of Luke 15, the prodigal son's father reached out to his son because he had repented. Confession is a great secret to reconciliation and success in our Christian walk. The many cases of divorce among Christians and unbelievers alike could have been averted if people would learn the simple principle of accepting and confessing our faults to one another. There is indeed power in confession; it is a tool of reconciliation.

In spite of David's sins, God called him "a man after my own heart" (Acts 13:22 NIV). The reason why David was blessed of God is that he was different in his reaction to his faults. He accepted blame and responsibility for his sins and iniquities, repented and confessed instantly.

I had an encounter with a colleague which brought the message of repentance and its effects home to me. I was supposed to understudy a colleague who was leaving her post for another job. She happened to be very mean to me and did not give me the coaching that I needed to take over the job. I made a complaint to our supervisor who questioned her about her behavior. Later on, she asked to talk to me alone in our office. She then told me how sorry she was for her behavior. Immediately, I felt a deep love, respect and appreciation reaching out from my heart to her and I felt compelled to embrace her. It was then that I understood what the Bible means when it says David was a man after God's own heart. Since David had a repentant and humble spirit, God's heart went out to him with a deep love and affection.

141

God knows all the secrets of our heart because He is the Author of our faith and has a record of anything that we have ever done, therefore, we should not try to hide any sin from Him. Like King David, we should live a life of transparency by accepting our faults and confessing them instantly to God or our fellow men. God said "My eyes are on all their ways; they are not hidden from me, nor is their sin concealed from my eyes" (Jeremiah 16:17 NIV). It would be naïve on our part to try to cover up our sins.

God Forgives

Scripture assures us in I John 1:9 that "if we confess our sins, he is faithful and just and will forgive us our sins and purify us from all unrighteousness" (NIV). Confession is a prerequisite for forgiveness, salvation and deliverance. God is faithful to forgive us because He has promised to do so. In Isaiah 1:18a He promised, "Come now, let us reason together says the Lord. Though your sins are like scarlet, they shall be white as snow." God's relationship with David explains the depths of His unfathomable mercy and grace. We should always acknowledge our transgressions before the Lord. If we are full of sins and iniquities such as envy, greed, hate, anger, pride, lust, fornication and murder, then we shall be destroyed because these are evil spirits dwelling in us that will not inherit the kingdom of heaven (Galatians 5:19-21).

> **There is no substitute, and no amount of weeping, sorrowing, sentimentalism or fasting can take the place of confession.**

Nothing can take the place of confession. There is no substitute, and no amount of weeping, sorrowing, sentimentalism or fasting can take the place of confession.

Chapter 20

Prayer of Supplication

We are All Needy People

God has made an open invitation to everyone to come to Him with our requests and petitions. In Matthew 11:28 Jesus said, "Come to me, all you who are weary and burdened, and I will give you rest" (NIV). I once questioned a colleague about this verse: "Would someone who is not weary and burdened need to go to God or receive His Son Jesus Christ as the verse is implying?" He then responded with another question "Is there anyone who is not weary and burdened?" It then dawned on me that everyone needs God: the rich, poor, black, white, brown, famous, infamous, those in authority and those under authority.

The fact that everyone needs God reveals our insufficiency in ourselves. The Word of God declares in John 15:5c "Apart from me you can do nothing" (NIV) and the prophet Isaiah said, "All men are like grass, and all their glory is like the flowers of the field. The grass withers and the flowers fall" (Isaiah 40:6b,7a NIV). God has put these limitations on man so that no one can exalt himself and claim that he or she is equal with God or better than his fellow man. Like Paul, God has given everyone a thorn in the flesh, "a thorn of insufficiency" in order to humble us and draw us to Him for help. This reminds me of President George Bush's televised speech saying that, "Since September Eleven, people have been drawn to God in prayer to ask for wisdom." Make no mistake, the president knows that he cannot make it without wisdom from above.

After the disaster caused by Hurricane Katrina in New Orleans and its surrounding areas in August 2005, President Bush commented on national television that, "We have been belittled by the forces of nature." He and all government officials were left in a state of confusion and did not know how to handle the situation.

God is wise. Everybody is needy and we all need God - Africans, Asians, Europeans, Australians, North and South Americans alike without exceptions. One has money to buy a bed but does not have sleep. Another has sleep but has no money to buy a bed. Another has money, bed and sleep but feels very lonely and may even contemplate suicide.

We have no control over our appearance, no matter how hard we think we are trying with plastic surgery and face-lifts. We did not choose our race and for that matter our skin color or hair texture. A wise person would say that my color, hair texture and appearance were determined by my DNA. The question is, Who created the DNA anyway? Mr. Wise, did you play any role?

Power, education, beauty, popularity and financial position do not solve marital problems, family issues, social problems and health issues. The rich encounter marital problems, family issues, social problems and health issues, as do the poor.

It doesn't matter who we are, we all have no control over aging, death, natural disasters, misfortune and even sickness -no matter what our financial position and the amount of medical technology one can employ. In the twinkle of an eye tens of thousands of people perished in Asia by the tsunami in December, 2004. As a matter of fact, no one will escape death and we have no solution to the problem of death which makes us even more insufficient.

In a West African country, Ghana, there once lived a fetish priest by the name Okomfo Anokye of the Ashanti tribe. This man is believed to have commanded a golden stool from the clouds which has been a symbol of unity and strength among the Ashanti tribe. He planted a sword in the earth and no one has been able to remove the sword until today. He is purported to have promised that he was going to die and after his death, he would return with a concoction which would prevent death. This event took place in the eighteenth century and he has been dead until now and has not returned with the concoction.

It is only our Savior and Lord Jesus who said, "Therefore doth my Father love me, because I lay down my life, that I might take it again. No man taketh it from me, but I lay it down of myself. I have power to lay it down, and I have power to take it again. This commandment have I received of my Father" (John 10:17,18). This prophecy came to pass because Jesus died, was buried and on the third day He rose triumphantly from the dead and declared, "All power is given unto me in heaven and in earth" (Matthew 28:18b). He is the only one who has power over death.

Drawing the Line

Someone may rightly ask, "The Christians also encounter all these problems, so what is the difference?" The difference is, in Christ we have fulfillment, in that:

- Our sins have been washed by His blood (Revelation 7:14b).

- We have redemption through His blood (Colossians 1:14).

145

- We have peace that passes human understanding (Philippians 4:7).

- We are complete in Him through love (1 John 4:12).

- We have power to become the sons of God (John 1:12).

- We have fullness of joy (John 15:11).

- Above all, we are hidden with Christ in God (Colossians 3:3).

- We have hope of eternal life (Titus 1:2).

- God has to endorse or sanction anything that will ever befall His children (Job 1:12).

It is written in Revelations 21:2-4, "And I John saw the holy city, new Jerusalem, coming down from God out of heaven, prepared as a bride adorned for her husband. And I heard a great voice out of heaven saying, Behold, the tabernacle of God is with men, and he will dwell with them, and they shall be his people, and God himself shall be with them, and be their God. And God shall wipe away all tears from their eyes; and there shall be no more death, neither sorrow, nor crying, neither shall there be any more pain: for the former things are passed away." The promises go on and on, too many to be enumerated.

Full Assurance

The following scriptural verse gives us assurance and hope. In I John 5:14,15 it is written, "And this is the confidence that we have in him, that, if we ask any thing according to his will, he heareth us: And if we know that he hear us, whatsoever we ask, we know that we have the petitions that we desired of him." God is not a respecter of persons; He has made an open invitation for all to come to Him with our burdens - sickness, marital, financial, educational, job and other spiritual problems.

God is our only source of hope and without His help there is nothing we can do. He forgives our sins and, therefore, there is nothing to hinder us from receiving from Him. George Bennard who composed "The Old Rugged Cross" in 1912 sung, "I will cling to the old rugged cross and exchange it some day for a crown." Let us hold on firmly to God, cling to Him in hope and know that He will answer our prayers. We should always bear in mind that "God has not promised us a smooth journey, but a safe arrival" quoted from ABC documentary by Mrs. Ruth Graham. Habakkuk 2:3 says, "For the vision is yet for an appointed time, but at the end it shall speak, and not lie: though it tarry, wait for it; because it will surely come, it will not tarry."

Forms of Supplication

The following forms of supplication have been used in the Bible and could be applied in varying forms as the Holy Spirit leads us:

- ***Throwing a Fleece (A Sign or Confirmation from God)***

Gideon needed assurance from God in order to

go to battle with the Midianites. He, therefore, used a fleece to prove God in order to convince himself of God's protection (Judges 6:37-39).

• **_Promise of an Offering to God_**

Hannah was barren and in her supplications to God, she made a vow that if God would give   her a child, she would give the child back to God as a dedication to the service of God (I Samuel 1:11,12).

• **_Giving an Offering in Advance_**

In 1999, while in South Africa, my wife and I had our shop put up on sale for almost one whole year. Many prospective buyers had come and gone without any success. We then decided that we would leave the shop in the care of a friend and travel because we were relocating to another country for good. We had bought our air ticket and were scheduled to travel the following day when we received a phone call. This caller said, "I spoke to you about a month ago concerning my interest in your shop. I am out of town but please hold on. Whatever time I arrive tonight, I will come and see you." We postponed our trip and after our meeting on the next day, we were paid by a cashier's check the following day.

Earlier on in the week we had donated an amount of one thousand rands in South African currency (equivalent to about two hundred dollars) to TBN during a Praise-A-Thon appeal for funds and we prayed for God's help to sell the property. A few days later I had dreamed that a sack was being sent to me through the skies. I understood in the dream that it was a present but I had no idea what kind of present it was.

All these events took place in about a week or two. The cashier's check amounted to about a hundred times that of our donation (Luke 6:38).

- ***Pleading Your Case with God (Putting God in Remembrance):***

King Hezekiah put God in remembrance of his service to Him when he was told by the prophet Isaiah that he was going to die. He reminded God of his dedication and faithfulness to Him and King Hezekiah wept bitterly before God. God "repented" of His decision and added fifteen more years to his life (II Kings 20:1-6; Isaiah 43:26).

Chapter 21

Prayer of Intercession

*T*he Apostle Paul wrote to Timothy his son in the Lord, "I urge, then, first of all, that requests, prayers, intercession and thanksgiving be made for everyone - for kings and all those in authority, that we may live peaceful and quiet lives in all godliness and holiness. This is good, and pleases God our Savior, who wants all men to be saved and to come to a knowledge of the truth" (I Timothy 2:1-4 NIV).

Paul saw the need for believers to pray and intercede for everyone, especially for kings and all those in authority because leaders affect the lives of millions of people and the mistakes they made have led millions of souls into destruction. The mistakes of individual people may cost them their own lives, but for leaders and those in authority, their mistakes can affect us all, affect our children, and even have generational consequences. It is, therefore, imperative that we as believers respond and act with all the urgency that intercession deserves.

> The mistakes of individual people may cost them their own lives, but for leaders and those in authority, their mistakes can affect us all, affect our children, and even have generational consequences.

Wars in various places are a result of the activities and decisions of leaders, kings and those in authority in many places around the world such as Iraq, Afghanistan, Sierra Leone, Liberia, Kosovo, Congo, Sudan and many other countries that have had wars.

We Have Authority

God has committed the responsibility of determining the course of events in this world into our hands. We, as the light and salt of the world, should pray and take control of events in our world. We should dispel the darkness in the world by our light and preserve the world from decay and corruption by our saltiness. Until we pray, God cannot act because He is a God of principles. In the gospel of Mark 6:7 it is written, "And he called unto him the twelve, and began to send them forth by two and two; and gave them power over unclean spirits." Likewise, Matthew 18: 18,19 says, "I tell you the truth, whatever you bind on earth will be bound in heaven, and whatever you loose on earth will be loosed in heaven. Again, I tell you that if two of you on earth agree about anything you ask for, it will be done for you by my Father in heaven" (NIV). The power has been given to us. The only way we can access the power is by prayer.

> **Until we pray, God cannot act because He is a God of principles.**

There is so much for which to intercede that the list could go on and on. We are to pray for our Christian leaders so that they can preach the Word of God with all boldness. The Apostle Paul prayed, "Now, Lord, consider their threats and enable your servants to speak your word with great boldness" (Acts 4:29 NIV). We should also pray for our nations, communities and families. The Bible says that we are Kings, Priests and Ambassadors of Christ (Revelation 1:6, II Corinthians 5:20).

Kings are responsible for their nations, and we as believers should be responsible for our nations. Priests intercede for other people, and so we are responsible to intercede for our communities and families. Ambassadors represent the interests of their governments around the world and we should, therefore, represent the interest of the kingdom of God on earth and ensure that the expectations of the kingdom are established and carried out.

If there was ever a time to intercede, it is now. The return of the Lord Jesus Christ is nearer now than ever. Almost all the prophecies concerning the end times have been fulfilled. It is obvious that the September Eleven deaths at the World Trade Center included some Christians. The Word of God says that, "My people are destroyed from lack of knowledge" (Hosea 4:6 NIV). The knowledge of prayer of intercession will save our lives, and we will live in peace as the Bible says. If we do not pray and intercede, we cannot have peace and shall likewise perish. It is the prayer of some believers that has preserved our world until now.

"The king's heart is in the hand of the Lord; he directs it like a watercourse wherever he pleases" (Proverbs 21:1 NIV). As we intercede for those in authority, God begins to direct their steps so that the enemy will not determine what takes place on earth, and then we shall dwell in peace. The Psalmist said, "The kings of the earth take their stand and the rulers gather together against the Lord and against his Anointed One. 'Let us break their chains,' they say, 'and throw off their fetters'" (Psalm 2:2,3 NIV). Kings and those in authority could be a tool in the devil's hands to hinder the spread of the gospel. Let us now arise and stand up to the challenges facing us in our world today in order that we will live peaceful and quiet lives, and in the end God may be glorified.

I Can't Be Bothered!

A West African tale is told of a Tortoise, a Liane (plant) and a Bird. The Bird was perching on a treetop one afternoon and was as usual, chirping its tunes. The Tortoise was also enjoying the cool of the forest floor but sensing danger asked the Liane to tell the Bird to stop singing because they could all be in serious trouble. The Liane replied, "I can't be bothered. What has the Bird's singing got to do with me?" The Tortoise continued to plead with the Liane to tell the Bird to be quiet but all was to no avail. A hunter was busy going on his daily rounds looking for a prey. Attracted by the sound of the Bird he got closer, aimed and shot at it. The Bird went straight down and fell at the side of the Tortoise. The Hunter then went to fetch his catch, and to his joy and amazement, he found a Tortoise also lying at the spot where the Bird had fallen. He picked up the Bird, the tortoise, and looking up, saw the Liane. He quickly cut a long piece of the Liane that was dangling on the tree and with it tied the Tortoise and the Bird and off he went home happily with his catch. On the way, the Tortoise reminded the Liane, "I told you to tell the Bird to stop chirping, and now here we are in trouble."

In this present world, no one can say that "I am not concerned about what is going on around me and in the world." We cannot say that we have food, clothing and shelter, and we cannot be bothered. Many rich folk who lived around the World Trade Center in New York with big businesses were rendered homeless within minutes. They had lost everything and were in the soup lines of the Red Cross.

Let us rise from our sleep and slumber and pray in our authority given to us by God as individuals, groups, fellowships, churches and communities so that we shall not be overtaken by the enemy. Let us take some time off our busy and tight schedules to pray and intercede for God's intervention; otherwise, we will not survive to enjoy the wealth and knowledge we think we are accumulating and acquiring. Intercession does not come easily to many Christian folks; therefore, churches and fellowships should engage their members to pray and intercede as they come together to worship the Lord because many people are Sunday worshippers.

A minister friend said rightly, "We have to pray for our enemies so that we shall live in peace." If we do not pray and defeat the enemy now, then the enemy will defeat us later. "But I tell you: Love your enemies and pray for those who persecute you" (Matthew 5:44 NIV). "The prudent see danger and take refuge, but the simple keep going and suffer for it" (Proverbs 27:12 NIV).

> **If we do not pray and defeat the enemy now, then the enemy will defeat us later.**

Bearing Each Others Burdens

Intercession was made for Peter while he was in prison, and God sent an angel to deliver him miraculously to the surprise of the disciples (Acts 12:1-17). We should pray for one another especially in difficult times such as in sickness and in persecutions when we cannot help ourselves, and our faith grows weak. It is imperative that we look for trusted prayer partners who will always stand and pray with us. It is very easy to feel lost and lonely in a church, especially in the mega churches of today where no one will even know your name let alone what you are going through. Prayer partners can give the required support to be able to overcome and stand in time of your need.

There is a Reward

Whenever we sow our time, effort and substance into other people's lives, God rewards us by meeting our personal needs. As we intercede for others, we will definitely be blessed of God. When King Solomon asked God for wisdom to rule his nation in order that the children of Israel will be judged rightly and be blessed, God rewarded him by giving him all that he had not asked for in addition to what he requested. In II Chronicles 1:10-12, King Solomon prayed:

> "'Give me wisdom and knowledge, that I may lead this people, for who is able to govern this great people of yours?' God said to Solomon, 'Since this is your heart's desire and you have not asked for wealth, riches or honor, nor for the death of your enemies, and since you have not asked for a long life but for wisdom and knowledge to govern my people over whom I have made you king, therefore wisdom and knowledge will be given you. And I will also give you wealth, riches and honor, such as no king who was before you ever had and none after you will have'" (NIV).

Chapter 22

Prayer of Warfare

God Fights Our Battles

In II Chronicles 20:17, God assured Jehoshaphat, "You will not have to fight this battle. Take up your positions; stand firm and see the deliverance the Lord will give you, O Judah and Jerusalem. Do not be afraid; do not be discouraged. Go out to face them tomorrow, and the Lord will be with you" (NIV). God has promised on many occasions to fight our battles for us, some of which we are not even aware of. He protects us from evil while we are sleeping, in our going out and coming in and He saves us from diverse kinds of evil. God declared that He will fight against those who fight against us (Psalm 35:1). He will be an enemy to your enemies and will oppose those who oppose you (Exodus 23:22). He said, "If anyone does attack you, it will not be my doing; whoever attacks you will surrender to you...no weapon forged against you will prevail, and you will refute every tongue that accuses you. This is the heritage of the servants of the Lord, and this is their vindication from me" (Isaiah 54:15,17 NIV).

Just imagine a God who knows the very imaginations, machinations, plots, schemes, devices and all the plans of your enemy fighting on your behalf. There would be no room left for the enemy to maneuver and win his fight against you.

We know from these Bible verses that God does fight many of our battles for us, and throughout the history of the children of Israel there were many instances when God fought for them. Many people have testified of how God has delivered them miraculously from their troubles. I have personally had experiences where God delivered me from evil plots in my dreams, and these manifested the very next day in the natural. God is still in the business of fighting for His people. He has not changed, He is still the same yesterday, today and forever (Hebrews 13:8).

We Also Fight

There is a battle going on in the spiritual realm that has to be fought by us. God has not promised us a walk over the devil but a fight. However, we know that the greatest victory has been won on the cross of Calvary. There are certain battles in our lives that God expects us to fight out with the weapons that He has made available for us. We are in partnership with God. He does His part, and we have to do our part. For instance, God willed to give the land of Canaan to the children of Israel, but they did not possess the land without a fight. They were confronted with many enemies that they had to battle like the Jebusites, Edomites, Perizites, Amorites, Amalekites, Hittites, Hivites, Moabites and Girgashites.

> **God has not promised us a walk over the devil but a fight.**

The Psalmist proclaimed, "Praise be to the Lord my Rock, who trains my hands for war, my fingers for battle" (Psalm144:1 NIV). We are fighting an enemy who does not rest. He is always on the move seeking for whom he may devour (I Peter 5:8). We, therefore, have to be prepared at all times knowing that we are on a battlefield. We also have to fight our "Edomites," "Perizites" and many other "…ites" who stand in the way of our breakthrough.

God has set open doors before us. He has blessed us with all spiritual and material blessings, but the devil opposes us and makes it difficult for us to inherit and enjoy our possessions. Paul realized this truth and said, "But I will stay on at Ephesus until Pentecost, because a great door for effective work has opened to me, and there are many who oppose me" (I Corinthians 16:8,9 NIV).

The Word of God commands us to cast out demons, cast down imaginations, pull down the strongholds of the enemy and bring into captivity every thought to the obedience of Christ (II Corinthians 10:3-5). There are battles that have to be fought and won by us with the weapons of prayer and fasting made available to us.

Daniel interceded for his nation Israel that God should pardon their sins and remove their desolation. He fasted and prayed for three weeks before the Lord. Daniel 9:2-5,17-19 reads:

> In the first year of his reign I Daniel understood by books the number of the years, whereof the word of the Lord came to Jeremiah the prophet, that he would accomplish seventy years in the desolations of Jerusalem. And I set my face unto the Lord God, to seek by prayer and supplications, with fasting, and sackcloth, and ashes: And I prayed unto the Lord my God, and made my confession, and said, O Lord, the great and dreadful God, keeping the covenant and mercy to them that love him, and to them that keep his commandments; We have sinned, and have committed iniquity, and have done wickedly, and have rebelled, even by departing from thy precepts and from thy judgments:...Now therefore, O our God, hear the prayer of thy servant, and his supplications, and cause

159

thy face to shine upon thy sanctuary that is desolate, for the Lord's sake. O my God, incline thine ear, and hear; open thine eyes, and behold our desolations, and the city which is called by thy name: for we do not present our supplications before thee for our righteousness, but for thy great mercies. O Lord, hear; O Lord, forgive; O Lord, hearken and do; defer not, for thine own sake, O my God: for thy city and thy people are called by thy name.

God answered his prayers the very first day he purposed in his heart to seek the Lord, but the prince of Persia stood in the way of the messenger of God and prevented Daniel from receiving answers to his prayers. Michael, the archangel, had to come to the aid of the messenger of God. The angel said, "Do not be afraid, Daniel. Since the first day that you set your mind to gain understanding and to humble yourself before your God, your words were heard, and I have come in response to them. But the prince of the Persian kingdom resisted me twenty-one days. Then Michael, one of the chief princes, came to help me, because I was detained there with the king of Persia" (Daniel 10:12,13 NIV).

In some situations we have to persevere in prayers as Daniel did because the forces of darkness stand in the way of our breakthrough. We should never give up under such circumstances knowing that the Lord who has begun a good work in us will bring it to pass (Philippians 1:6).

There are many evil forces in the spiritual realm that are fighting and opposing the children of God and working against God's creation. There are many territorial spirits that control and influence the lives of people. These evil forces control and influence continents, nations, areas, communities, tribes, races, families, individuals and even operate within the church. Lifestyles, habits and attitudes that do not conform to God's standards are the workings of evil spirits. Homosexuality, drug abuse, crime, promiscuity and civil wars have destroyed the lives of millions around the globe. God is depending on us to do warfare, to pull down the strongholds of the enemy and liberate the captives. For this reason the son of man came to set the captives free (Luke 4:18). We have to do what is humanly possible, and God will do what is humanly impossible.

The Potency of the Word

During times of warfare, God has made available to us weapons that cannot be resisted by the enemy. Whilst praying and fasting we should remember to use the Word of God like Jesus did; "it is written." The word of God is a Hammer, it is Fire (Jeremiah 23:29), it is Quick, it is Powerful, it is Sharp, it is a Sword (Hebrews 4:12), it is a Balm of Gilead and a Medication (Jeremiah 8:22), it is Life and it is Spirit (John 6:63). Fasting and praying in the name of Jesus and applying the Blood of Jesus empowered by the Holy Ghost will invoke and infuse your prayer with an anointing and faith that will break every yoke and remove mountains, straighten up crooked paths, fill up the valleys, pull down strongholds and bring into captivity every thought to the obedience of Christ.

161

Chapter 23

Prayer of Thanksgiving, Praise and Worship

After enjoying the sweet, comforting, strengthening, holy and divine presence of God, our faith reaches such a height that thanking God becomes a natural outcome knowing that He will answer and grant our requests because He is a faithful Father. Let thanks and appreciation flow from the depths of our hearts because we are privileged to have someone who is Almighty, All Knowing and All Sufficient to be our Father. It is this that gives us the confidence to thank Him even for those things we have not seen because of who God is. Hebrews 11:1 says, "Now faith is being sure of what we hope for and certain of what we do not see" (NIV). As I have already indicated, thanking God is the highest form of faith that anyone could ever exhibit. When we thank the Lord, we also praise Him affirming our confidence in Him for what He has done and what He is capable of doing. Praise will automatically usher us into worshipping God for who He is.

Now that we have illumination about what prayer is, it becomes more of a joy than the burden the devil has tried to make it appear to be. I wish to end by saying that we should always know that the Holy Spirit may have His way sometimes; therefore, we should be flexible and open to the leadership of the Spirit in our prayers.

Hearing from God

I would like to address this aspect of prayer by sharing my personal experience. I was getting ready to go to church one Sunday morning but I only had thirty minutes left to prepare. I was about to shave my face, but before I started, I heard a voice saying to me that I should spend the rest of the time praying instead of shaving. I know that the devil would never ever tell me to pray so I obeyed and prayed. When I went to church that morning, there had been some developments and I knew then that if I had not prayed, things would not have gone well for me. Based on this experience, I would like to make the following suggestions that would help us to become more sensitive to God's voice:

- God will never say anything contrary to His Word.

- The devil will never say anything to us that will bring glory to God. For example, he will never tell us to pray, study God's Word, have faith in God, be patient, forgive, etc.

- God can speak at any time during prayer, not only at the end of prayer.

- God speaks in many ways and sometimes through special gifts such as Word of Knowledge.

- Just as we can talk to God at anytime we want to, God can also talk to us anytime, for example, when driving, on the job, at school, even in the restroom, not only during our prayer or study

164

time (more on this under Chapter 31 "How Does God Talk Back To Us?").

- God may speak to us through a specific means which may differ from one person to another; for example, God spoke to Joseph through dreams, Balaam through the mouth of his donkey and Daniel through dreams, visions and writing on the wall.

- Finally, if you are not sure of God's direction, give yourself time, and do not make a decision because with time God will unfold His plan and direction for your life.

We grow in our sensitivity and our understanding of God's voice as we get to know Him better with maturity just as we get to know other people's voices when we become more familiar with them as time goes by.

As you develop a relationship or talk to God often, you will know His voice. As an analogy, let us consider someone calling on the phone; as you pick up the receiver, you begin to wonder who it is that is calling. If the caller is someone you talk to all the time, you immediately recognize the person because you are familiar with the voice even though the caller might not mention his or her name. As it is written in John 10:4,5, "And when he putteth forth his own sheep, he goeth before them, and the sheep follow him: for they know his voice. And a stranger will they not follow, but will flee from him: for they know not the voice of strangers." You will be able to discern the voice of God with time. I believe that these suggestions will make a seemingly difficult subject understandable to many people.

NOTES:

PART SIX
Principles of Prayer

Chapter 24

Does God Answer Prayer?

*W*ho has not questioned "Why?" Who has not lamented, and who has not grieved? Why me, why this, why that? Everyone has had a midnight hour when you were burdened, rolled and turned in your bed with a heavy heart and had tears run down your cheeks. Problems had surrounded and overwhelmed you and you did not know the way out. When you were at the verge of finding a solution to one problem, there came another and many times you have asked, "Does God care?" I have asked this question many times. Job had a similar experience. For example, Job 1:15-19 records:

> "And the Sabeans fell *upon them*, and took them away;
> yea, they have slain the servants with the edge of the
> sword; and I only am escaped alone to tell thee. While
> he *was* yet speaking, there came also another, and said,
> The fire of God is fallen from heaven, and hath burned
> up the sheep, and the servants, and consumed them;
> and I only am escaped alone to tell thee. While he *was*
> yet speaking, there came also another, and said, The
> Chaldeans made out three bands, and fell upon the
> camels, and have carried them away, yea, and slain
> the servants with the edge of the sword; and I only am
> escaped alone to tell thee. While he *was* yet speaking,
> there came also another, and said, Thy sons and thy

daughters *were* eating and drinking wine in their eldest brother's house: And, behold, there came a great wind from the wilderness, and smote the four corners of the house, and it fell upon the young men, and they are dead; and I only am escaped alone to tell thee."

The Apostles also asked the same question, "carest thou not that we perish?" But what was Jesus' response? He came to their rescue by saying, "Peace be still" (Mark 4:39b).

On another occasion the disciples asked Jesus, "Master, who did sin, this man, or his parents, that he was born blind? Jesus answered, Neither hath this man sinned, nor his parents: but that the works of God should be made manifest in him" (John 9:2). Sometimes we get frustrated and discouraged because the devil keeps telling us that our sin has brought misfortune on us.

Let us examine an incident in the Bible to try to find out if misfortune is always a consequence of sin. We read from scripture that Job was upright and blameless, but he had his share of calamities, disappointments and frustrations. People who should have stood for him turned their backs and condemned him. While he was being told of evil that had befallen his house, a messenger was bringing another report of a misfortune. The enemy attacked him with a barrage of problems with the intent of crushing, breaking, undoing and paralyzing him in an attempt to separate him from the God of Israel in whom he trusted.

What do we do as believers when we are faced with tragic and unpleasant experiences? Psalm 46:10a says, "Be still, and know that I am God." The main objective of the enemy is to separate us from the love of God. All he needs from us is to steal our faith in Christ, because we can do wonderful exploits if we have faith in the Lord. We should remember what the Apostle Paul wrote to the Church in Rome, "Who shall separate us from

170

the love of Christ? shall tribulation, or distress, or persecution, or famine, or nakedness, or peril, or sword...." (Romans 8:35). He concludes by saying, "In all these things we are more than conquerors through him that loved us" (Romans 8:37). Let us be persuaded in our walk with the Lord that neither death nor life nor things present or things to come shall be able to separate us from the love of Christ.

In times of trials or crisis remember to pray and encourage yourself in the Lord because the truth is that if the devil has an agenda, God also has a plan. All that you are going through will work out for your good according to Paul in the book of Romans 8:28. Likewise the Psalmist says, "He will call upon me, and I will answer him; I will be with him in trouble, I will deliver him and honor him" (Psalm 91:15 NIV).

Let me share a praise report that will encourage you whenever you are going through a trial. A Pastor friend of ours was being evicted from his house under very unprepared circumstances. We were contemplating him spending some time with us until he found a place. Little did he know that God had prepared a place, bigger, nicer and even more presidential than he had ever thought. Another friend lost his job after working for many years. After staying jobless for a while, he was appointed to be a director of an organization, and he is now contemplating starting his own business. I am agreeing with James that we have to count it all joy when we fall into diverse temptations; knowing this, that the trying of our faith works patience. But let patience have her perfect work, that you may be perfect and entire, wanting nothing (James 1:2-4).

We know from Scripture that God answers prayers, and He wants us to call upon Him at all times. In order to understand God better and know whether He is interested in answering our prayers, let us consider an illustration of how a responsible earthly father addresses issues concerning his children because Jesus on many occasions used earthly illustrations to explain heavenly or spiritual principles.

We all know too well that an earthly father is protective of his children, is proud and "jealous" of them and dreams of the best in terms of providing education, nourishment, clothing, shelter, good health, etc. for his children. Listen to what God says about the good earthly father and how all these cannot be compared to how He feels and thinks about us. In Matthew 7:11, He said "If you, then, though you are evil, know how to give good gifts to your children, how much more will your Father in heaven give good gifts to those who ask him" (NIV). We know that God is our Father in heaven according to Matthew 6:9, and all the good that we think we are desiring for our children is not comparable to what God desires for us and is planning to do. He said, "For I know the thoughts that I think toward you, saith the Lord, thoughts of peace, and not of evil, to give you an expected end" (Jeremiah 29:11).

The problem we have with God as I see it, is that God is not a God of our "timing." When we have made up our minds about the manner and the time frame we think God should work, He shows us a different calendar and agenda for our lives. That is why there is a need for us to be patient in every tribulation. Looking back at history and the dealings of God with men, one realizes that God's timing has always turned out to be the best.

Jesus Christ had His share of experiences with trouble, rejection, disappointments, tragedy and eventual death. At that point, He reacted in the same manner that we do. He requested that the cup (trial, test and affliction) should pass from Him in spite of the fact that He knew God had called Him for that assignment. Scripture tells us that because He has been tempted, He is able to succour (keep, strengthen, preserve) us through temptation until we are victorious (Hebrews 2:18).

The reason why we can rely and depend on God's Word is that He has no limitations, and nothing can hinder or stop Him from doing what He has pledged or purposed to do. Numbers 23:19 says, "God is not a man, that he should lie, nor a son of man, that he should change his mind. Does he speak and then not act? Does he promise and not fulfill?" (NIV).

I have identified six ways by which God answers or responds to prayer. They are:

A.　Yes

B.　No

C.　No with An Alternative

D.　Wait

E.　Permissive Will

F.　No Answer (Silent Heaven)

We will now look at examples from Scripture to examine the various ways that God answers prayer. However, we should bear in mind that whichever way God chooses to answer our prayers is always the best for us because He is Omniscient. He is for us and not against us.

Chapter 25

Yes, God Answers Prayer

*I*n those days Hezekiah became ill and was at the point of death. The prophet Isaiah son of Amoz went to him and said, 'This is what the Lord says: Put your house in order, because you are going to die; you will not recover.' Hezekiah turned his face to the wall and prayed to the Lord, 'Remember, O Lord, how I have walked before you faithfully and with wholehearted devotion and have done what is good in your eyes.' And Hezekiah wept bitterly. Before Isaiah had left the middle court, the word of the Lord came to him: 'Go back and tell Hezekiah, the leader of my people, "This is what the Lord, the God of your father David, says: I have heard your prayer and seen your tears; I will heal you. On the third day from now you will go up to the temple of the Lord. I will add fifteen years to your life"'" (II Kings 20:1-6a NIV).

In this account we see God answering Hezekiah's prayer instantly. The Bible declares in Isaiah 43:26, "Put me in remembrance: let us plead together: declare thou, that thou mayest be justified." Hezekiah put God in remembrance concerning his faithfulness to Him and he was justified. Hezekiah's father Ahaz was an idol worshiper, but when Hezekiah succeeded his father on the throne, he brought religious reformation to the kingdom of Judah. II Kings 18:6 says, "He held fast to the Lord and did not cease to follow him; he kept the commands the Lord had given Moses" (NIV). He cleaned Judah of idol worshipping; that is why he was able to confidently approach God and put Him in remembrance. What would the end of Hezekiah have been like if he had given up on God? Had he not put God in remembrance, he would have perished. Likewise we should not give up on anything until God gives His last Word. It is important, however, that we walk in faithfulness and do what is pleasing in God's eyes as Hezekiah did; without doing so we cannot have the confidence to go before the Lord and plead our case.

"And Jabez called on the God of Israel, saying, Oh that thou wouldest bless me indeed, and enlarge my coast, and that thine hand might be with me, and that thou wouldest keep me from evil, that it may not grieve me! And God granted him that which he requested" (I Chronicles 4:10). Jabez called upon the Lord in his time of need and the Lord granted what he asked for.

On many occasions Jesus responded instantly to the needs of people. He met people's needs out of compassion. In Luke 7:11-15 it is recorded,

> "Soon afterward, Jesus went to a town called Nain, and his disciples and a large crowd went along with him. As he approached the town gate, a dead person was being carried out - the only son of his mother, and she was a widow. And a large crowd from the town was with her. When the Lord saw her, his heart went out to her and he said, 'Don't cry.' Then he went up and touched the coffin, and those carrying it stood still. He said, 'Young man, I say to you, get up!' The dead man sat up and began to talk, and Jesus gave him back to his mother" (NIV).

Has it ever occurred to us to call upon the Lord to bring the dead back to life? This faith practice has almost become a thing of the past. Has God changed? I heard the testimony of the General Overseer, Rev. Dr. Stephen Gyermeh of the Church of the Living God in Hyattsville, Maryland who prayed for three hours for his dead mother, and she was restored back to life and has lived to her ninetieth birthday.

Jesus also responded to the faith of people. A centurion said to Jesus, "That is why I did not even consider myself worthy to come to you. But say the word, and my servant will be healed....When Jesus heard this, he was amazed at him, and turning to the crowd following him, he said, 'I tell you, I have not found such great faith even in Israel.' Then the men who had been sent returned to the house and found the servant well" (Luke 7:7,9,10 NIV).

The woman who had an issue of blood for twelve years and had spent all that she had said to herself, "If I may but touch his garment, I shall be whole. But Jesus turned him about, and when he saw her, he said, Daughter, be of good comfort; thy faith hath made thee whole. And the woman was made whole from that hour" (Matthew 9:21,22).

These Biblical accounts reveal that God responds to prayer and these are recorded as examples for us to know that God is able to meet our needs. He is the same God. He never changes. "Jesus Christ the same yesterday, and today, and forever" (Hebrews 13:8). He said, "For I am the Lord, I change not" (Malachi 3:6a). Let us call upon Him.

Chapter 26

Sometimes God Answers 'No' to Our Prayer

God sometimes answers 'No' to our prayers and we cannot comprehend all the ways of God. James H. Evans, Jr. noted "...the outsider's view, which sees the indeterminacy of the text as evidence of its divine origin in the experience of the holy. We cannot understand why a loving Father should answer "No" to some of man's dire needs." According to Evans, "the indeterminacy of the text is evidence of its divine origin. If so, then there is no doubt that the source of the text is divine and therefore beyond our cognition."

In our imaginations we expect God to answer all our prayers in the affirmative, but we should not forget that God is always for us and not against us. He assures us in Jeremiah 29:11, "For I know the thoughts that I think toward you, saith the Lord, thoughts of peace, and not of evil, to give you an expected end." God can never be wrong; it is up to us to exercise absolute faith and confidence in Him.

Some of the Apostles of old were martyred. John Foxe in his book on church history, *Foxe's Christian Martyrs of the World*, wrote concerning the death of Peter and Paul, "The apostle Peter was condemned to death during the first persecution, although some say he escaped. It is known that many Christians encouraged him to leave the city, and the story goes that as he came to the city's gate, Peter saw Jesus coming to meet him. 'Lord, where are you going?' Peter asked. 'I am come again to be crucified,' was the answer. Seeing that this suffering was understood, Peter returned to the city, where Jerome tells us he was crucified head down at his own request, saying he was not worthy to be crucified the same way his Lord was. Paul also suffered under this persecution when Nero sent two of his esquires, Ferega and Parthemius, to bring him to his execution. They found Paul instructing the people and asked him to pray for them, so they might believe. Receiving Paul's assurance that they would soon be baptized, the two men led him out of the city to the place of execution, where Paul was beheaded."

Why? Why? Why?

"El Tablazo looked so close. Too close. It happened so fast. Exploding into the jagged 14,000-foot peak, the DC-4 disintegrated with a metallic scream. What was left of the Avianca Airline flight bound for Quito, Ecuador flamed crazily down the mountainside into a deep ravine. One awful moment illuminated a cold Colombian dark mountain in the night, then the darkness returned. And the silence.

Before leaving the airport earlier that day, a young New Yorker named Glenn Chambers hurriedly scribbled a note on a piece of paper he found on the floor of the terminal. The scrap was part of a printed advertisement with a single word, "Why?" sprawled across the center. Needing stationery in a hurry, Chambers scrawled a note to his mother around the word in the middle. Quickly folding this last minute thought, he stuffed it in an envelope and dropped it in a box. There would be more to come, of course. More about the budding of a lifelong dream to begin a ministry with the Voice of the Andes in Ecuador.

But there was no more to come. Between the mailing and the delivery of Chambers' note, El Tablazo snagged his flight and his dreams from the night sky. The envelope arrived later than the news of his death. When his mother received it, the question burned up at her from the page - Why? It is the question that hits first and lingers longest. Why? Why me? Why not? Why this?" This story is told by Charles R. Swindoll as quoted in Biblical Preaching by Haddon W. Robinson.

Jesus commanded us to pray to the Lord of the harvest so that He would send workers to the field (Matthew 9:38). Glenn offered himself for the service of the Lord, but to our astonishment the Lord of the harvest who is Sovereign and Almighty did not protect Glenn on his missionary journey to Ecuador. As a matter of fact, God did not grant him traveling mercies and, therefore, he died tragically and miserably in the plane crash. A Christian may fall sick and believers will pray and seek God for His intervention, but unfortunately God answers No, and the child of God dies as a result. God declared, "'For my thoughts are not your thoughts, neither are your ways my ways,' declares the Lord. 'As the heavens are higher than the earth, so are my ways higher than your ways and my thoughts than your thoughts'" (Isaiah 55:8,9 NIV).

We will examine the deaths of our Lord Jesus Christ and what it accomplished, examine the deaths of some believers and other martyrs and the aftermath of their deaths. We will also search the Scriptures to find out what it says about such misfortunes in the life of a Christian.

Jesus Christ

Jesus Christ was crucified on Calvary and His disciples were discouraged, however, He rose on the third day as He had prophesied. On the day of Pentecost, the Holy Ghost descended on the disciples in the upper room at Jerusalem as Jesus had promised and they were emboldened from then on. The supernatural power of the Holy Ghost started to manifest in the lives of the Apostles and many were saved and baptized. About three thousand souls were added to the church when Peter preached and miraculous deliverance and healings began to take place (Acts 2:41).

Through the death of Jesus our sins have been forgiven and we have been reconciled back to God, for it is written "without shedding of blood there is no remission" (Hebrews 9:22b). Because of the shed blood, Gentiles and Jews alike have received salvation. Multitudes around the globe have been saved, delivered and healed through His sacrificial death on the cross. In I Corinthians 1:18 it is also written, "For the preaching of the cross is to them that perish foolishness; but unto us which are saved it is the power of God." It is because of the death and resurrection of Christ that we have peace and hope of eternal life. I Corinthians 2:8 says, "Which none of the princes of this world knew: for had they known it, they would not have crucified the Lord of glory." If the devil knew that the death of Jesus was going to spell his defeat and doom, he would have advised himself. The death of Jesus could never have been in vain.

Missionary (Horatio Spafford)

The story is told of a missionary, H. G. Spafford, while sailing to Africa on an evangelistic mission, received a telegram from his wife that all four of his daughters died in a shipwreck. Later on, as Spafford passed the area where his daughters died, in his grief and sorrow, the Holy Spirit inspired him to compose the song, "It is Well with My Soul" in 1873:

"When peace, like a river, attendeth my way,
When sorrows like sea billows roll;

Whatever my lot, Thou has taught me to say,
It is well, it is well, with my soul.
It is well, with my soul,
It is well, with my soul,
It is well, it is well, with my soul."

Although Spafford lost his four daughters, the song which resulted from the tragedy has healed many broken hearts, comforted many sorrowful people, revived many souls, millions have been blessed and generations to come will be blessed by his song.

Stephen

The Apostle Paul persecuted the Church before his conversion. The Bible records that he went from house to house and caused many people to be imprisoned. Stephen was martyred because of Saul's persecution and influence, and it was through the death of Stephen that Saul was converted. As he journeyed to Damascus to continue with his persecution of believers, God intervened by revealing Himself to Saul and he was converted and later became Paul The Apostle as a result of his encounter with the Lord. Many people were converted through Paul's ministry because he sold his life out for the gospel of Christ (Acts 8:1-4, 9:1-16).

Paul wrote thirteen epistles which have brought consolation, salvation, healing, deliverance, peace and comfort to many hearts. Tertullian said of the Martyrs, "The blood of the Martyrs is the seed of the Church." The deaths of many martyrs have brought about the religious freedoms that are enjoyed around many parts of the world today.

William Tyndale

William Tyndale, the "Father of the English Bible" who was martyred in the 16th century, was the first person to translate the Bible from the original languages to English and this has been of tremendous help in bringing millions to salvation. "His dream was to translate the Scriptures into the language of the common man. Speaking one day to a church leader, he said, 'If God spare my life, ere many years I will cause a boy that driveth the plough shall know more of the Scripture than thou doest.'"

"William Tyndale was arrested in May 1535 and remained in prison for more than sixteen months. On October 6, 1536, outside Antwerp, Tyndale was strangled and burned at the stake. He died as he lived – with the burden of the English people on his heart. His last words were 'Lord, open the King of England's eyes.'"

The translators of the King James version used his translation as the basis of their historic work. It would have taken many years for some of us to learn the original languages in order to comprehend what the Bible says and we could not have had a personal relationship with the Lord.

Martin Luther King Jr.

During one of the televised anniversaries of the death of Martin Luther King Jr., a Baptist Theologian and Political Activist, Andrew Young, a former U.S. Ambassador to the U.N., said of him, "Martin triumphed in death even more than when he lived. His death brought about desegregation and affirmative action." The political freedoms that we enjoy are a result of people who have laid down their lives such as Martin Luther King Jr., not forgetting that political freedoms have contributed to the religious freedoms of our time.

O Death, Where is Your Sting?

Death has served as a reminder to humans of our depravity and made us conscious of that fact so that we may humble ourselves before God in order that we will prepare to meet Him, and this has caused many sorrowing people to repent and turn to the Lord. The September Eleven deaths were a wake-up call which brought unity within nations and among nations and turned millions of hearts to God for salvation. It brought self-awareness, rededication, commitment and to many people, a determination to win the battle against the devil. The December 2004 deaths in Sri Lanka and the surrounding nations was another wake-up call, and we hope that people will realize the need to serve God in truth.

Besides what death accomplishes in the natural, a child of God is promised a crown of righteousness and eternal life after death. The Apostle Paul wrote to Timothy saying, "I have fought the good fight, I have finished the race, I have kept the faith. Now there is in store for me the crown of righteousness, which the Lord, the righteous Judge, will award to me on that day - and not only to me, but also to all who have longed for his appearing" (II Timothy 4:7,8 NIV). All these martyrs had finished the race and had kept the faith. Paul wrote to the people of Corinth in I Corinthians 15:54-57 saying:

"When the perishable has been clothed with the imperishable, and the mortal with immortality, then the saying that is written will come true: 'Death has been swallowed up in victory.' 'Where, O death, is your victory? Where, O death, is your sting?' The sting of death is sin, and the power of sin is the law. But thanks be to God! He gives us the victory through our Lord Jesus Christ" (NIV).

185

When our perishable bodies have put on the imperishable and when our mortal body is clothed with immortality, death will no longer have dominion over us. Then we will no longer experience death because the immortal body cannot be corrupted by death. The sting of death will be broken, cancer, diabetes, stroke, Parkinson's disease, etc. will no longer have power over us and all things will be new.

Searching through Scriptures and from practical observations and the testimonies of the martyrs discussed above, I am convinced that the death of a child of God is never in vain, but it is in God's plan because He allows it. Psalm 116:15 says, "Precious in the sight of the Lord is the death of his saints" (NIV). Revelations 14:13 says, "Then I heard a voice from heaven say, 'Write: Blessed are the dead who die in the Lord from now on.' 'Yes,' says the Spirit, 'they will rest from their labor, for their deeds will follow them'" (NIV).

Jesus has tasted death for us all, and He promised that He will be with us until the end of the world. He is with us even when we are going through death (Matthew 28:20). He will not leave us alone and what is more, II Corinthians 5:8b says, "To be absent from the body, is to be present with the Lord." Death is not the end; it is the birth of a new life with the Lord for eternity. It is a transport to heaven. The New York Times interviewed Franklin Graham of Billy Graham Evangelical Association, regarding the Tsunami. Franklin responding to the issue of death said, "Death is the portal that transfers us from this life to the next."

> **Death is not the end; it is the birth of a new life with the Lord for eternity.**

A few months before the publication of this book, my mother passed away. It was and still is the most painful experience

I have ever gone through. I wept bitterly because I had dedicated this book to her and I had many good thoughts of her. I was forced under the circumstance to change the dedication to read as "My Late Mother." What a devastation it was to me! At that point the Spirit of God dropped the verse from Revelations 14:13 into my spirit which says, "Then I heard a voice from heaven say, 'Write: Blessed are the dead who die in the Lord from now on.' 'Yes,' says the Spirit, 'they will rest from their labor, for their deeds will follow them'" (NIV).

Then I remembered how my mother had lived an exemplary life. I could not recall my mother being angry at any time in the real sense of the word. I had never personally seen her quarrel or have strife with anyone during all the time that I lived close to her before I relocated, and that was more than three decades. She was a mother to her sister's and brother's children, a mother to her friend's children and a mother to anyone who fitted into the mold of a son or a daughter. She was great, wonderful and a heroine.

During an interview with Bill Clinton, on the Oprah Winfrey Show, the former president said that he had learned from the African American churches that we all have a "Home Going" and he had concluded his book, "My Life," by saying that he is preparing for this inevitable event. Through my mother's death, the message has come crystal clear to me that death is certain and we all have a "Home Going." The fact that the verse in Revelation concludes by saying "and their deeds shall follow them" brought me comfort and the message that this is the time to preach and teach the Word of God more than ever before. I started writing a tribute about my mother with much confidence, because I knew then that my mother's deeds would follow her and the need for all of us to live lives worthy of praise came strongly to me.

All that I have written concerning death was more or less ratified and I want to end by quoting Max Cleland, a veteran of the Vietnam War, who, giving his speech from his wheelchair at the Democratic Convention of 2004 in Boston with two of his legs amputated said, "I have lost greatly but there are great things ahead to fight for and win."

Chapter 27

God May Answer 'No' But with an Alternative

The Apostle Paul was used mightily of God and wrote thirteen Epistles. He sent his handkerchief to heal the sick and raised the dead, but he had a thorn in his flesh. He called upon the Lord on three occasions to take away the thorn, but God did not remove it. In the end Paul said, "To keep me from becoming conceited because of these surpassingly great revelations, there was given me a thorn in my flesh, a messenger of Satan, to torment me" (II Corinthians 12:7 NIV). God did not take away the thorn but gave him grace to endure.

The type of thorn that Paul suffered in his flesh is not known exactly but we do know that it was unpleasant for him. God in His own wisdom decided not to remove it for a good and just reason. Paul wrote, "But he said to me, 'My grace is sufficient for you, for my power is made perfect in weakness.' Therefore I will boast all the more gladly about my weaknesses, so that Christ's power may rest on me. That is why, for Christ's sake, I delight in weaknesses, in insults, in hardships, in persecutions, in difficulties. For when I am weak, then I am strong" (II Corinthians 12:9-10 NIV).

Jesus Christ agonized in prayer in Gethsemane that God should take away the cup from Him, however, God did not remove the cup but rather sent an angel to strengthen Him (Luke

189

22:41-43).

There have been countless testimonies of people who have prayed to God about their hearts desires and thought that God had "disappointed" them because they did not receive answers to what they had asked God for. Later they realized that God had given them a better treat than what they had desired.

Chapter 28

God May Tell Us to Wait

*M*any times we do not have instant answers to our prayers. God deals with us as individuals and He has no blueprint by which He responds to our prayers. There are several examples in the Bible of different ways by which God responded to the requests of His servants which means that there is a need for Christians to wait patiently for God in some situations. Every parent will bear testimony that you do not give everything that your child asks for instantly. The child has to wait for the appropriate time.

Waiting, from a Biblical point of view has several connotations. It means waiting patiently for God to come to our aid in His own time. It also means fasting before God or praying to the Lord about a burden. It could also mean trusting God to answer our prayers.

Zechariah and Elizabeth prayed for a child for many years until they were past the age of fruitfulness. Luke 1:5-7 tells of their story: "In the time of Herod king of Judea there was a priest named Zechariah, who belonged to the priestly division of Abijah; his wife Elizabeth was also a descendant of Aaron. Both of them were upright in the sight of God, observing all the Lord's commandments and regulations blamelessly. But they had no children, because Elizabeth was barren; and they were both well along in years" (NIV).

The Bible records that they were righteous before God, but they waited for many years before God answered their prayers. The time of waiting for God is a very unpleasant period. It is during that time that our faith is tested. Our patience, endurance and courage are also brought to the test. The Bible has a record of many people who suffered the problem of barrenness. They waited for many years before God came to their rescue, but in all those instances, God intervened and made them fruitful. The Bible talks about Sarah, Rebekah, Rachel, the Shunammite woman and Hannah. These women were all barren, but God blessed them with fruitfulness, not one was left out. We have consolation from the testimonies of these women. They show us that we need patience and absolute trust in God. James 1:4 says "But let patience have her perfect work, that ye may be perfect and entire, wanting nothing."

You may have been praying to the Lord for a spouse, healing, deliverance, fruitfulness, about your child on drugs, an unsaved husband or wife, a job; just wait for Him, never relent in your pursuit for a solution because He will answer in His appointed time. We have assurances from the Word of God. Isaiah 40:31 says, "But they that wait upon the Lord shall renew their strength; they shall mount up with wings as eagles; they shall run, and not be weary; and they shall walk, and not faint." "For the revelation awaits an appointed time; it speaks of the end and will not prove false. Though it linger, wait for it; it will certainly come and will not delay" (Habakkuk 2:3 NIV).

Like Paul, let us fight the good fight of faith, never giving up because He is faithful to do what He has promised. Your case has been opened. He is working on it and will call for your hearing, so wait for His call.

> **Your case has been opened. He is working on it and will call for your hearing, so wait for His call.**

Chapter 29

We May Be Living In God's Permissive Will

The story of Barak in the fourth chapter of the book of Judges tells how Deborah the Prophetess had prophesied concerning the children of Israel that Barak should lead the Israelite army to battle against Sisera, the commander of Jabin, king of Canaan. God had told Deborah that He would give Sisera and his army into Barak's hands. Barak did not heed the words of the prophetess and said to her, "…If thou wilt go with me, then I will go: but if thou wilt not go with me, then I will not go" (Judges 4:8). Deborah went with Barak to war and they defeated the enemy. However, Barak did not get the glory; instead Jael, the wife of Heber the Kenite, was given the glory by killing Sisera as was prophesied by Deborah. The will of God was for Barak to defeat and kill Sisera, but due to his disobedience, God permitted him to go with Deborah to war and defeat the Canaanites but the glory went to Jael.

Many times Christians live under the permissive will of God due to disobedience, especially in issues regarding relationships with the opposite sex. Many people claim to be waiting upon the Lord for a life partner, but the truth of the matter is, they have made up their minds already as to who they want to marry, or love. Sometimes people set standards for themselves and all of these hinder them from hearing the voice of God. God allows them to follow their egos which will not be His perfect will for their lives.

No Answer (Silent Heaven)

Sometimes there is no answer to your prayer or there seems to be no answer coming forth, and everything looks dead around you. You do not even feel that God is saying "no" to your prayer, neither do you hear an inner voice. When you pray, the prayer seems to bounce back to you from the ceiling. All circumstances around you do not give any indication of God's response; when you fast it feels like God has turned His back on you and the Heavens seem to be silent.

Whenever you find yourself in this predicament, do not make any decisions, just wait for God. If you decide to go ahead of God to make any moves, you may end up regretting your actions. Give yourself time and God will eventually unfold His plan or answer to your prayers and His will, will be done. Continue to stay your mind on God and He will keep you in perfect peace. The prophet Isaiah declares "Thou wilt keep *him* in perfect peace, *whose* mind is stayed *on thee*: because he trusteth in thee" (Isaiah 26:3).

Chapter 30

Why Do The Righteous Suffer?

God permits His children to go through suffering and persecutions for a purpose. He is Sovereign and Almighty but He does not always seem to come to our aid when we most need Him. Dr. Morris Cerullo, an Evangelist, once said, "God is a God of Plan, a God of Purpose, a God of Objectivity and a God of Design." We almost always want God to act according to our plans, but we should understand that God's plans and purposes are His will for our lives. We should fit ourselves into God's plan and purpose for our lives through prayer and His Word, instead of God fitting into our plans. Another important attribute of God is that He is very patient, but we have a tendency to want quick and instant answers from God. Searching through the Bible, I have identified some of the reasons why God allows His people to go through suffering.

> We should fit ourselves into God's plan and purpose for our lives through prayer and His Word, instead of God fitting into our plans.

In Order To Know Who God Is

The children of Israel knew God as the God of their fathers - the God of Abraham, Isaac and of Jacob, but they did not know Him as their own God and that He was so real and was concerned about their suffering. There is a difference between knowing the God of the Bible and knowing Him as your personal deliverer. In Exodus 3:13,14 it is recorded, "And Moses said unto God, Behold, *when* I come unto the children of Israel, and shall say unto them, The God of your fathers hath sent me unto you; and they shall say to me, What is his name? what shall I say unto them? And God said unto Moses, I AM THAT I AM: and he said, Thus shalt thou say unto the children of Israel, I AM hath sent me unto you." After God had delivered the Israelites by His mighty hand they were pursued by Pharaoh's chariots and his horsemen. They were also trapped by the Red Sea in front and were literally squeezed and crushed between two "mountains" with no way of escape. It was at this darkest moment in their lives and history that they experienced the greatest deliverance and manifestation of God's power that has ever been recorded in the history of man (Exodus 14:10-30). The question is: What did this deliverance do in the lives of the Israelites?

1.   It made them to understand the whole concept of God and to know Him and who He is. Exodus 14:31 says, "And Israel saw that great work which the Lord did upon the Egyptians: and the people feared the Lord, and believed the Lord, and his servant Moses."

2.   There was no way that they would have known the power of God without having to go through this test.

Let us ask ourselves - Would we ever have known God on a personal level if we never experienced His deliverance and mercies? The answer I believe is 'No.' Suffering is therefore a "tool" that draws us closer to God and causes us to know Him and who He is. Someone may ask, "Do we have to go through suffering in order to know God?" The answer again is 'No,' but I believe that everyone has a kind of "thorn in the flesh" that will draw us to God. In order to bring clarity on this subject, here are a few examples of what I mean by thorn in the flesh: sickness, marital problems or failure in marriage, low self-esteem, bondage to a kind of sin, an unruly child, financial problems, crisis in the family such as death, loss of job and the like. These are a few examples of what I mean by thorn in the flesh. Men are heavily laden with diverse kinds of "thorns" which draw us to God.

To Purify Us As Gold

In order to obtain gold metal from the ore, it suffers from physical, chemical and in some cases biological attacks or hardships. The physical attacks include large tension forces, compressive forces, excessively high temperatures and strong electric fields. Additionally, the chemical attacks include leaching reagents, de-sorption reagents, electro-winning chemical activities and smelting chemical actions. Furthermore, biological actions such as the use of bacteria in the process of bio-oxidation is used in some cases for gold processing.

I Peter 1:6,7 says, "In this you greatly rejoice, though now for a little while you may have had to suffer grief in all kinds of trials. These have come so that your faith - of greater worth than gold, which perishes even though refined by fire - may be proved genuine and may result in praise, glory and honor when Jesus Christ is revealed" (NIV). The writer of Peter makes an analogy of the trial of our faith being as gold refined by fire, but he says that our faith is more precious than gold. Like gold our faith is attacked by spiritual and natural forces, such as trials in the home, job, school, church, financial, health, family, etc. These forces attack our faith; but in the process, our faith through manifold temptations is refined and produces praise and honor and glory at the appearing of Jesus Christ which will in the end result in our salvation (I Peter 1:8). These forces mold and refine our character, give us experience and strengthen or toughen us.

A Butterfly's Lesson

One day, a small opening appeared in a cocoon; a man sat and watched for the butterfly for several hours as it struggled to force its body through that little hole. Then, it seemed to stop making any progress. It appeared as if it had gotten as far as it could and it could not go any further.

So the man decided to help the butterfly: he took a pair of scissors and opened the cocoon. The butterfly then emerged easily. But it had a withered body, it was tiny and had shriveled wings. The man continued to watch because he expected that, at any moment, the wings would open, enlarge and expand, to be able to support the butterfly's body, and become firm. Neither happened! In fact, the butterfly spent the rest of its life crawling around with a withered body and shriveled wings. It never was able to fly.

What the man, in his kindness and his goodwill did not understand was that the restricting cocoon and the struggle required for the butterfly to get through the tiny opening, were God's way of forcing fluid from the body of the butterfly into its wings, so that it would be ready for flight once it achieved its freedom from the cocoon.

Sometimes, struggles are exactly what we need in our life. If God allowed us to go through our life without any obstacles, it would cripple us. We would not be as strong as we could have been. Never been able to fly. I asked for Strength...and God gave me difficulties to make me strong. I asked for Wisdom... and God gave me problems to solve. I asked for prosperity...and

*God gave me a brain and brawn to work. I asked for Courage...
and God gave me obstacles to overcome. I asked for Love...and
God gave me troubled people to help. I asked for Favors...and
God gave me Opportunities. I received nothing I wanted...But I
received everything I needed.*

Like the pressure which pumps fluid into the butterfly's
wings, pressure, crisis, hardships, tests and trials will "pump"
character, courage, faith and experience into your spirit as the
Apostle Paul said, "Therefore I take pleasure in infirmities,
in reproaches, in necessities, in persecutions, in distresses
for Chirst's sake: for when I am weak, then am I strong" (II
Corinthians 12:10).

To Prove Our Faith In God

One of the reasons why the righteous suffer is that we have
faith in God, which is a very precious asset. Our salvation is by
faith and anything we shall ever accomplish in our righteousness
is by faith. Reading through the eleventh chapter of Hebrews will
illuminate one's mind as to how our "fathers" conquered through
faith and for that matter the importance of faith in our walk with
the Lord. The fact that we are accepted by God through the blood
of Christ is all because of our faith. Hebrews 11:6 tells us that,
"Without faith it is impossible to please God" (NIV).

God allows the devil to test us because He knows that we
have faith, and He has trust and confidence in us that we shall
be able to stand firm on His Word and triumph. Looking at the
trials of Job closely reveals that God had "confidence" in Job and
wanted to prove Job's faith in Him, and also that Job did not serve
God because he was blessed of Him. Job 1:8,9 reads, "Then the
Lord said to Satan, 'Have you considered my servant Job? There
is no one on earth like him; he is blameless and upright, a man
who fears God and shuns evil.' 'Does Job fear God for nothing?'

Satan replied" (NIV).

The devil persecuted Job so much that he lost everything he had ever possessed. He lost his children and all his belongings, he was afflicted with sores, and "his wife said to him, 'Are you still holding on to your integrity? Curse God and die!'" Listen to Job's reply, "You are talking like a foolish woman. Shall we accept good from God, and not trouble…?" (Job 2:9,10 NIV). In Job 13:15a he said, "Though he slay me, yet will I trust in him…." You know as much as I do that Job was eventually restored. His latter days were more blessed than his beginning because he had faith in God. Faith brought back everything he had lost. Oh! How precious faith is. The Bible says in Hebrews 11:2, "For by it the elders obtained a good report," and there is a line of people in the same chapter of Hebrews who made great accomplishments through faith. The devil knows the importance of our faith so he is after us. Faith is the greatest, faith is the key. This is why James said, "Count it all joy when ye fall into divers temptations; Knowing this, that the trying of your faith worketh patience. But let patience have her perfect work, that ye may be perfect and entire, wanting nothing" (James 1:2-4).

The devil pursues the children of God and tries to bring hardships to cause us to give up or renounce our faith or else to compromise. He makes sure that he inflicts pain on believers for the simple reason that we have identified with Christ through faith. The Apostle Paul said, "We are hard pressed on every side, but not crushed; perplexed, but not in despair; persecuted, but not abandoned; struck down, but not destroyed" (II Corinthians 4:8,9 NIV). We will not bow to the whims and caprices of the devil or compromise our faith because the Word of God declares in Luke 1:45, "And blessed is she that believed: for there shall be a performance of those things which were told her from the Lord." God will perform what He has promised concerning His children. He is faithful, reliable, dependable, trustworthy, and

He will never disappoint us. Johnson Oatman, Jr. realized this truth concerning the Word of God and he wrote:

No Not One

There's not a friend like the lowly Jesus
No, not one! No, not one!
Jesus knows all about our struggles
He will guide till the day is done

Our faith causes us to walk in the righteousness of God and apply "Kingdom" principles within the world (kingdom) of Satan because we are not of his world. This same faith releases the anointing, the power and the glory of God upon us, which makes the devil feel very uncomfortable and he unleashes his powers of darkness (demon spirits) to come against us and pursue our lives, on the job, in the home, in our marriage, at school, in our body, finances and sometimes he shows up from within the Church. Jesus Christ who is the righteousness of the righteous was hated and disliked by His own people, was falsely accused, spat upon, rejected of men, persecuted and finally crucified for the very reason that He is the author and finisher of our faith. The devil is after our precious faith.

The Point of Eli Eli Lama Sabachthani

Jesus Christ suffered many things at the hands of His own people. "He came unto his own, and his own received Him not..." (John 1:11). He went through persecution and eventually ended up on the cross. He was forsaken and rejected by His people and His disciples alike with nobody to help. Peter had promised earlier that if all men would forsake Him, he would never leave Him and would even lay down his life for Him. When the time came for Peter to prove his love for Jesus, he swore with an oath saying "I do not know the man" (Matthew 26:72b). Jesus felt that even God had forsaken Him and while on the cross, He cried out, "Eli, Eli, lama sabachthani? [(Matthew 27:46)] that is to say, My God, my God, why hast thou forsaken me?"

Many servants of the Lord have at one time reached this point in their life. We are not alone in our trials. We can recall the experience of Job, David and Naomi. Job said in his grief, "He tears me down on every side till I am gone; he uproots my hope like a tree. His anger burns against me; he counts me among his enemies" (Job 19:10,11 NIV). David also cried, "My God, my God, why have you forsaken me? Why are you so far from saving me, so far from the words of my groaning?" (Psalm 22:1 NIV). Ruth's mother-in-law had this to say, "'Don't call me Naomi,' she told them. 'Call me Mara, because the Almighty has made my life very bitter. I went away full, but the Lord has brought me back empty. Why call me Naomi? The Lord has afflicted me; the Almighty has brought misfortune upon me'" (Ruth 1:20,21 NIV).

As a child of God you will be persecuted, you will go through trials, through the fire, through the waters and through the storms. Like our Master and Lord Jesus we will at one time or another reach a position where we will find our backs against the wall with no way of escape, no help coming forth and knowing under our circumstance that God seems to have forsaken us.

Like Jesus, Job, David, Naomi and other people of God we may also come to the point where we say, "Eli Eli lama sabachthani." My wife and I have been in that situation on several occasions. When all seems to be lost, let us stay with the Lord Jesus Christ and continue to have hope in Him. For it is written, "And hope maketh not ashamed; because the love of God is shed abroad in our hearts by the Holy Ghost which is given unto us" (Romans 5:5). God has also promised that we will not be tempted above that which we will be able to stand. "There hath no temptation taken you but such as is common to man: but God is faithful, who will not suffer you to be tempted above that ye are able; but will with the temptation also make a way to escape, that ye may be able to bear it" (I Corinthians 10:13).

To Whom Shall We Go?

When all hope is gone and you have no one to turn to, when you feel that under your circumstance God has forsaken you although He has promised that He will never leave you nor forsake you and when all is darkness around you and you cannot see the way forward, remember to remain where you are even in your hopelessness with the Lord Jesus Christ and never give up. We do not know why God does not deliver us when we are being chased by the "lion." We do not know why God does not deliver us when the lion pins us down and allows it to swallow us before He comes to our rescue. We do not know why God allows us to literally "die" sometimes before He restores us.

God will show up at the nick of time. I believe He chooses to do that in order to teach us His faithfulness and prove His greatness and power. Michael W. Smith, the song writer composed "There She Stands," the lyrics say:

"When the night, Seems to say, All hope is lost, Gone away, But I know, I'm not alone, By the light, He stands…"

God will show up when all hope is lost. He is by your side. Many of the disciples of Jesus had forsaken Him because some of His sayings were too hard for them to receive. John 6:67-69 says, "Then said Jesus unto the twelve, Will ye also go away? Then Simon Peter answered him, Lord, to whom shall we go? thou hast the words of eternal life. And we believe and are sure that thou art that Christ, the Son of the living God."

Beside Jesus there is no one else to whom we can turn. Even those who you think will never turn their backs on you may fail you. Jesus alone has the words of comfort. He is the Prince of Peace. He alone is Lord. He alone has the words of eternal life and He is the Christ, the Savior of our souls. We should always bear in mind that the delays of God are not denials. He may delay in order to teach us patience, prove our faith, build our character and strength or reveal His power on our behalf.

When Jesus got news that Lazarus was sick, He delayed going to visit him. After Lazarus died, He hesitated and arrived at Lazarus' tomb on the fourth day when the dead body was decomposing. When He arrived at the scene, He brought Lazarus back to life. According to Jewish beliefs at the time, the spirit of the dead hovered around for three days before departing. If Jesus had arrived before the end of the third day, they might have thought that Lazarus was not dead after all since his spirit had not departed. Jesus might have waited until the fourth day to prove to the disciples that He has power over death, hell and the grave. When Jesus finally made it plain that Lazarus had died, He told His disciples in John 11:15, "And I am glad for your sakes that I was not there, to the intent ye may believe." Jesus was building the faith of the disciples so that they could take over His ministry after He was gone.

Don't give up if God does not show up when you most need Him. Just stay with Him. He may delay for a purpose, of course God has a reason. Even if you lose hope, continue to stay with Him because He will surely show up when you are no longer expecting Him. You are in God's plans and purposes. Psalm 46:10a says, "Be still, and know that I am God..." He says we should understand that He is not man, but God Almighty. Therefore, we should be patient, wait for Him, trust Him and He will prove Himself to be God on our behalf. He understands our tendency to lose hope. Even our Lord Jesus Christ has been in that state before. When your condition is as hopeless as death, that is when the Lord will manifest His power. John 12:24 says, "Verily, verily, I say unto you, Except a corn of wheat fall into the ground and die, it abideth alone: but if it die, it bringeth forth much fruit." God is building your faith so that you can also be an encouragement to someone.

Sometimes your condition should look like "dead" or reach a state of hopelessness in order for God's glory to be manifested. You cannot receive a miracle unless your situation demands a miracle. Like the woman with the issue of blood, she received a miracle because her situation demanded a miracle. "But the God of all grace, who hath called us unto his eternal glory by Christ Jesus, after that ye have suffered a while, make you perfect, stablish, strengthen, settle you. To him be the glory and dominion for ever and ever. Amen" (1 Peter 5:10,11).

Even our Lord Jesus had to die before all the power, glory and dominion was given to Him. He had to go through pain in order to gain and reconcile us back to God. When you reach the point where all hope is lost, just wait for the Lord, even in your hopelessness, for it is written, "Many are the afflictions of the righteous: but the Lord delivereth him out of them all" (Psalm 34:19). Bear in mind that the afflictions are many, not few and God delivers us not from some of our afflictions but from all of them.

The Word of God assures us in Hebrews 12:2 that, "Jesus (is) the author and perfecter of our faith." We all know the functions of an author; he keeps a detailed record of events. He updates information and reorganizes it. He removes and adds information. Jesus, the author of our faith, is keeping record of all the faithful works that we have done. Our labors in the Lord are all recorded. When we err, He records it; but when we repent, He removes it from our records. I have always thought of how a computer keeps information, and that makes me get a clear picture of how Jesus has kept records of our works of faith. Whenever we think hope is lost, Jesus steps in and perfects our faith.

> **Whenever we think hope is lost, Jesus steps in and perfects our faith.**

Some versions of Scripture say that, "He is the author and finisher of our faith." When we find ourselves in devastating circumstances where our faith fails, Jesus steps in and finishes or makes our faith complete. When the going gets tough, let us hold on and never give up because Jesus is tougher than our toughest circumstances. Remember the end of Job, which was more blessed than his beginning.

> **When the going gets tough, let us hold on and never give up because Jesus is tougher than our toughest circumstances.**

David is referred to as a friend of God and He wrote most of the book of Psalms. Naomi's daughter-in-law Ruth, was blessed of God, she is named in the genealogy of Jesus Christ and Naomi was honored in the end. Even Jesus went through the test and now He has a testimony that at the mention of His name every knee shall bow. It is true that without a test there will be no testimony, without a trial there will be no triumph, without a cross there is no crown, without pain there will be no gain and without a story there will be no glory. Blessed be the name of the Lord.

God Tests Our Faith

God may be testing our faith as He did in the life of Abraham. In the book of Genesis 22:1,2 we are told, "And it came to pass after these things, that God did tempt Abraham, and said unto him, Abraham: and he said, Behold, here I am. And he said, Take now thy son, thine only son Isaac, whom thou lovest, and get thee into the land of Moriah; and offer him there for a burnt offering upon one of the mountains which I will tell thee of." The next verse of the same chapter of Genesis tells us that Abraham rose up early in the morning and did as God had told him. He did not ask questions; neither did he argue. He even refused to mention this plan to his wife in order to avoid any opposition from her. God blessed Abraham so much because of his faith and obedience. God declared, I swear by myself that in blessing I will bless you (Genesis 22:16-18). Your faith is being tested. In the end, you will receive your blessing. Be strong!

To Keep Us Humble

The Apostle Paul had a thorn in his flesh and from all indications it was an unpleasant experience for him, so he sought the Lord to remove the thorn. Paul says in II Corinthians 12:7-10:

"To keep me from becoming conceited because of these surpassingly great revelations, there was given me a thorn in my flesh, a messenger of Satan, to torment me. Three times I pleaded with the Lord to take it away from me. But he said to me, 'My grace is sufficient for you, for my power is made perfect in weakness.' Therefore I will boast all the more gladly about my weaknesses, so that Christ's power may rest on me. That is why, for Christ's sake, I delight in weaknesses, in insults, in hardships, in persecutions, in difficulties. For when I am weak, then I am strong" (NIV).

Paul makes us understand that the reason God did not remove the thorn was to keep him humble. Suffering causes us to know that we are not in control of anything, not even our own

207

lives; therefore, our hearts cannot be lifted up into thinking that we have achieved anything by our own wisdom and power.

In Order to Learn Obedience

Our Lord Jesus Christ learned obedience through the many things He suffered. Hebrews 5:8,9 says, "Although he was a son, he learned obedience from what he suffered and, once made perfect, he became the source of eternal salvation for all who obey him" (NIV). If Jesus Christ who knew no sin suffered in order to learn obedience, how much more should we not learn obedience from our bitter experiences and sufferings. I can identify with the writer of Hebrews concerning the truth in this assertion because personally, through many afflictions I have learned obedience. The Word of God says that "he who spares the rod hates his son" (Proverbs 13:24 NIV). A child who lives under the discipline of the parents reaps the benefits of the discipline as opposed to a 'street child' who does not live under any kind of discipline.

To Know that God is a Deliverer, Healer and a Provider

God has a reason, purpose and plan for whatever He allows in the lives of His people. He allows His children to go through suffering in order for Him to show His greatness on their behalf. When God sent Moses to deliver the children of Israel from slavery in Egypt, He hardened Pharaoh's heart to show Himself mighty to the Egyptians and to the children of Israel. The Lord said to Moses in Exodus 7:3-5, "But I will harden Pharaoh's heart, and though I multiply my miraculous signs and wonders in Egypt, he will not listen to you. Then I will lay my hand on Egypt and with mighty acts of judgment I will bring out my divisions, my people the Israelites. And the Egyptians will know that I am the Lord when I stretch out my hand against Egypt and bring the Israelites out of it" (NIV).

The children of Israel had a tough time walking to freedom, but at the end of it all God used their suffering to prove Himself mighty in such a way that Pharaoh confessed that the God of Israel is indeed God. In Exodus 9:27 it is recorded, "And Pharaoh sent, and called for Moses and Aaron, and said unto them, I have sinned this time: the Lord is righteous, and I and my people are wicked." Pharaoh's magicians also saw the power of the God of Israel and they reported to Pharaoh that "this is the finger of God" (Exodus 8:19a NIV).

After all if we never fell sick, how could we have known and believed that God is our healer. He said in Exodus 15:26b, "...for I am the Lord, who heals you" (NIV). God is faithful and has promised that He will never leave or forsake us. "For the eyes of the Lord run to and fro throughout the whole earth, to show himself strong in the behalf of them whose heart is perfect toward him" (II Chronicles 16:9a).

God provided manna for the children of Israel in the desert. In the desert, Jesus multiplied food for thousands of people. Let us make our hearts perfect, and God will show Himself strong in our bad situations.

To Help or be an Encouragement to Others

God prepares us to be vessels of comfort to people who are sorrowing and hurting. II Corinthians 1:3,4 says, "Praise be to the God and Father of our Lord Jesus Christ, the Father of compassion and the God of all comfort, who comforts us in all our troubles, so that we can comfort those in any trouble with the comfort we ourselves have received from God" (NIV). When one has gone through an experience, he is better equipped to be of help to the person going through the same or similar experience.

For the Glory of God to be Revealed in Us

In the gospel of John, the disciples of Jesus asked saying, "Master, who did sin, this man, or his parents, that he was born blind? Jesus answered, Neither hath this man sinned, nor his parents: but that the works of God should be made manifest in him" (John 9:2,3).

The story is told of three Jewish men, Shadrach, Meshach and Abednego in the province of Babylon who refused to worship the golden image that King Nebuchadnezzar had set up. They were condemned to be cast into a burning fiery furnace but God sent His angel to deliver these young men who had trusted in Him.

"Then Nebuchadnezzar the king was astounded, and rose up in haste, and spake, and said unto his counsellors, Did not we cast three men bound into the midst of the fire? They answered and said unto the king, True, O king. He answered and said, Lo, I see four men loose, walking in the midst of the fire, and they have no hurt; and the form of the fourth is like the Son of God. Then Nebuchadnezzar came near to the mouth of the burning fiery furnace, and spake, and said, Shadrach, Meshach, and Abednego, ye servants of the most high God, come forth, and come hither. Then Shadrach, Meshach, and Abednego, came forth of the midst of the fire. And the princes, governors, and captains, and the king's counsellors, being gathered together, saw these men, upon whose bodies the fire had no power, nor was an hair of their head singed, neither were their coats changed, nor the smell of fire had passed on them.

Then Nebuchadnezzar spake, and said, Blessed be the God of Shadrach, Meshach, and Abednego, who hath sent his angel, and delivered his servants that trusted in him, and have changed the king's word, and yielded their bodies, that they might not serve nor worship any god, except their own God. Therefore I make a decree, That every people, nation, and language, which speak any thing amiss against the God of Shadrach, Meshach, and Abednego, shall be cut in pieces, and their houses shall be made a dunghill: because there is no other God that can deliver after this sort. Then the king promoted Shadrach, Meshach, and Abednego, in the province of Babylon" (Daniel 3:24-30).

The King saw the awesome power of God and blessed the God of Shadrach, Meshach and Abednego. When you are going through suffering or being persecuted for the reason of believing in the Lord Jesus or for walking in righteousness, wait and see God move on your behalf and His glory revealed in your life.

When We Go Through Persecutions and Difficulties We Gain Experience

Paul said, "Are they servants of Christ? (I am out of my mind to talk like this). I am more. I have worked much harder, been in prison more frequently, been flogged more severely, and been exposed to death again and again. Five times I received from the Jews the forty lashes minus one. Three times I was beaten with rods, once I was stoned, three times I was shipwrecked, I spent a night and a day in the open sea, I have been constantly on the move. I have been in danger from rivers, in danger from bandits, in danger from my own countrymen, in danger from Gentiles; in danger in the city, in danger in the country, in danger at sea; and in danger from false brothers. I have labored and toiled and have often gone without sleep; I have known hunger and thirst and have often gone without food; I have been cold and naked" (II Corinthians 11:23-27 NIV).

There are no problems that we have encountered that Jesus Christ and the Apostles did not also go through. In I Peter 2:21 we are reminded that, "To this you were called, because Christ suffered for you, leaving you an example, that you should follow in his steps" (NIV). Paul suffered many things as he labored for the Lord. Through the things he suffered, he was strengthened all the more to carry on the work of the ministry and God gave him grace to overcome all his trials. When we go through various trials and temptations, we gain experience and experience gives us hope to become victorious.

Romans 5:2-5 says, "through whom we have gained access by faith into this grace in which we now stand. And we rejoice in the hope of the glory of God. Not only so, but we also rejoice in our sufferings, because we know that suffering produces perseverance; perseverance, character; and character, hope. And hope does not disappoint us, because God has poured out his love into our hearts by the Holy Spirit, whom he has given us" (NIV).

The truth is that as long as we live, we will never graduate from the school of experience. With each passing day we experience new victories, successes, failures, disappointments, surprises, shocks and astonishments; however, God

> As long as we live, we will never graduate from the school of experience.

212

said we should trust Him. "And the one who trusts in him will never be put to shame" (Romans 9:33b NIV).

The Devil Wants to Separate Us From God

The devil does not care who you are because he attempted to trick Jesus himself after the Spirit of God had led Him into the wilderness. He tried to use his deception on Jesus when He ended His fasting. The Bible says, "And the devil said unto him, If thou be the Son of God, command this stone that it be made bread. And Jesus answered him, saying, It is written, That man shall not live by bread alone, but by every word of God. And the devil, taking him up into a high mountain, showed unto him all the kingdoms of the world in a moment of time. And the devil said unto him, All this power will I give thee, and the glory of them: for that is delivered unto me; and to whomsoever I will I give it. If thou therefore wilt worship me, all shall be thine" (Luke 4:3-7).

In the first place, the world does not belong to the devil because in the gospel of John it is written that, the same was in the beginning with God. All things were made by Him; and without Him was not anything made that was made (John 1:1-3). The devil is always armed with deceit, looking for a way to separate us from God. He seems to ask for very little things that will cause us to compromise. After Jesus had afflicted His soul through fasting, the devil wanted to prevent Him from fulfilling His assignment by surrendering to him. We need to finish the assignment given to us by God and not give in to the devil's temptations.

Chapter 31

How Does God Talk Back To Us?

*G*od is a Spirit: and they that worship him must worship him in spirit and in truth" (John 4:24). God is a spirit; therefore, we cannot talk to Him the same way we talk to our fellow man because we are made of three aspects namely spirit, soul and body. The question then is: "How does God talk to us knowing who God is?"

God speaks to us on three levels namely:

- To Our Body (Flesh)
- To Our Spirit (Inner Man)
- To Our Soul (Mind, Will, Emotions).

To Our Body

God Speaks Directly

In the beginning God spoke to His people Israel directly by divine means. "The Lord would speak to Moses face to face, as a man speaks with his friend" (Exodus 33:11a NIV). "When the Lord saw that he had gone over to look, God called to him from within the bush, 'Moses! Moses!' And Moses said, 'Here I am.' 'Do not come any closer,' God said. 'Take off your sandals, for the place where you are standing is holy ground.' Then he said, 'I am the God of your father, the God of Abraham, the God of Isaac and the God of Jacob. At this, Moses hid his face, because he was afraid to look at God" (Exodus 3:4-6 NIV). It is not normative for God to speak to us face to face. God does this only under divine circumstances.

God spoke audibly to Samuel. In I Samuel 3:3-9 God called Samuel and spoke audibly telling him about the judgment that was going to befall Eli's house because he did not restrain his household.

God Uses Human Vessels

In the natural realm God operates through man and quite often speaks to us through other people such as prophets, pastors, preachers, teachers, evangelists, friends, family members, brethren and sometimes even unbelievers.

When you study the Bible, it reveals the many vessels that God uses to speak to His people. God knows the words to speak to us at the right time, and He speaks through any vessel that is appropriate for the occasion and circumstances.

Through "Angels"

There are many examples both in the Old and New Testament of God speaking through angels. Acts 8:26 says, "And the angel of the Lord spake unto Phillip, saying, Arise, and go toward the south unto the way that goeth down from Jerusalem unto Gaza, which is desert."

God is still in the business of sending His angels in our way. God uses people to declare His statutes and fulfill His promises in our lives. For example, if you have been praying for

God to show Himself to you and then one day you came to your living room and found an angel with huge wings sitting on your sofa, what do you think would happen? You would most likely pass out immediately and may never regain consciousness. That is the reason why God uses people that we can relate to.

Once I had been praying about a job, and my wife happened to have a friend who worked in the department where I was desiring to work. My wife stopped by her house for an appointment, and it was then that she told her about an impending job fair by her department. I attended the job fair and was privileged to have a job. Since that day, we have never seen this friend of ours or heard from her for many years. I am convinced that she was our angel sent by God to inform us of the job fair in order for me to get the job I was praying about.

His Word

The second letter of Paul to Timothy 3:16 says, "All Scripture is God-breathed and is useful for teaching, rebuking, correcting and training in righteousness" (NIV). God usually speaks to us through His Word, therefore, Bible study is of utmost importance in our walk with the Lord. When we study God's Word and apply it in our lives, we are able to live out His image. The Word of God teaches us and saves us from so many forms of evil. The Word is a light which exposes evil, gives us direction and counsel so that we shall not fall as prey to the enemy who is desiring to destroy us. Psalm 119:105 says, "Your word is a lamp unto my feet, and a light unto my path." Coal miners wear their lamps on their head in order to see what is in the distance. God can speak through His Word on bumper stickers, billboards, etc.

God will speak to us in any way. For example, when you study or listen to the Word of God, He is able to speak to your marital problem even though the subject of the study is not on marriage. All this goes to prove the awesomeness of God's power and the fact that His Word is spirit and is life.

Circumstances

When we pray, God may not respond in any visible way, but through our circumstances we will know that God is responding to our prayers. For example, if your date or fiancée behaves in ways that you do not feel comfortable with all the time, or if he has the propensity of reaching for the gun in every little dispute, do not think that you will change him when you get married or vice versa. No one can change a person, it is only God who can bring about a change in someone's life. God is speaking to you through the negative attitude of your date; therefore, listen to Him. Otherwise you could one day become a news headline.

To Our Spirit

Our Inner Man (The Spirit within)

In John 10:4b-5, Jesus taught them saying, "and his sheep follow him because they know his voice. But they will never follow a stranger; in fact, they will run away from him because they do not recognize a stranger's voice" (NIV).

God speaks to us through our inner man, the spirit within. Sometimes we say, "I have a feeling that something is telling me to do this or that." That something could be the Holy Spirit speaking to you. As we commune with God, we will learn and know the voice of the Spirit.

God speaks through the Holy Spirit as we find in Acts 8:29, "Then the Spirit said unto Phillip, Go near, and join thyself to this chariot." We have to pray that the Lord will make our spirit sensitive in order to hear the voice of the Holy Spirit.

Gifts of the Spirit

Word of Wisdom

In I Kings chapter three, a story is told of two women who were arguing over who was the rightful mother of a child. One of these women had exchanged her dead child for the other woman's living child. So the case was brought before King Solomon for judgment.

> "And the other woman said, Nay; but the living is my son, and the dead is thy son. And this said, No; but the dead is thy son, and the living is my son. Thus they spake before the king. Then said the king, The one saith, This is my son that liveth, and thy son is the dead: and the other saith, Nay; but thy son is the dead, and my son is the living. And the king said, Bring me a sword. And they brought a sword before the king. And the king said, Divide the living child in two, and give half to the one, and half to the other. Then spake the woman whose the living child was unto the king, for her bowels yearned upon her son, and she said, O my lord, give her the living child, and in no wise slay it. But the other said, Let it be neither mine nor thine, but divide it. Then the king answered and said, Give her the living child, and in no wise slay it: she is the mother thereof" (I King 3:22-27).

Here we see the wisdom of God in demonstration in the life of King Solomon. This judgment could not have been possible without God's own divine wisdom and direction.

Word of Knowledge

John 1:45-50 says, "Phillip findeth Nathanael, and saith unto him, We have found him, of whom Moses in the law, and the prophets, did write, Jesus of Nazareth, the son of Joseph. And Nathanael said unto him, Can there any good thing come out of Nazareth? Philip saith unto him, Come and see. Jesus saw Nathanael coming to him, and saith of him, Behold an Israelite indeed, in whom is no guile! Nathanael saith unto him, Whence knowest thou me? Jesus answered and said unto him, Before that Philip called thee, when thou wast under the fig tree, I saw thee. Nathanael answered and saith unto him, Rabbi, thou art the Son of God; thou art the King of Israel. Jesus answered and said unto him, Because I said unto thee, I saw thee under the fig tree, believest thou? thou shalt see greater things than these."

Jesus knew about Nathanael before he ever met him. The Holy Spirit gives us revelation, knowledge and understanding of events and issues in our lives and in the lives of others.

To Our Soul

God also speaks to our minds. When you are thinking, reasoning, analyzing, assessing or asking questions in your mind, God may be speaking to your mind without you knowing. It does happen while we are in prayer that we tend to have imaginations and we think that it is our own thoughts. Our prayer may be interrupted by thoughts running through our mind, and we feel that it is our own imaginations. For example, the following analogy will help to explain this concept further; In the natural when a scientist is asking questions in his mind, analyzing and looking for a solution to a problem in an attempt to bring about an invention, to solve a scientific problem or medical problem, the solution may drop suddenly into his mind, and he thinks he is smart. Little did he know that God gave the solution for the benefit of all mankind.

When your back is against the wall and you do not know the way out of your predicament, suddenly God drops His Word into your mind. You become uplifted, faith rises in you and hope builds up. You begin to remember the past testimony in your life, peace and calmness begins to take control of your mind and immediately the problem begins to crumble down as it is written, I will keep you in perfect peace who's mind is stayed on me (Isaiah 26:3). Sometimes we say, "I have decided to go and see my brother or sister, so and so, for advice concerning a financial need, health or marital crisis." Little did we know that God has provided the solution or answer to that person purposely for you. It was not your will or decision; it was God's.

Dreams and Visions

God speaks to us through dreams and visions. In Numbers 12:6, "he said 'Listen to my words: When a prophet of the Lord is among you, I reveal myself to him in visions, I speak to him in dreams'" (NIV). In my personal walk with the Lord I have come to know that God speaks through dreams. Many people of God have also testified that God speaks to them through dreams and visions.

"This is how the birth of Jesus Christ came about: His mother Mary was pledged to be married to Joseph, but before they came together, she was found to be with child through the Holy Spirit. Because Joseph her husband was a righteous man and did not want to expose her to public disgrace, he had in mind to divorce her quietly. But after he had considered this, an angel of the Lord appeared to him in a dream and said, 'Joseph, son of David, do not be afraid to take Mary home as your wife, because what is conceived in her is from the Holy Spirit'" (Matthew 1:18-20 NIV). God directed Joseph and Mary through dreams concerning Jesus' conception and throughout his childhood.

God spoke to the three wise men through a dream. In Matthew 2:12 it is written, "And having been warned in a dream not to go back to Herod, they returned to their country by another route" (NIV).

God spoke to Joseph through dreams most of the time. For instance Genesis 37:5 says, "Joseph had a dream, and when he told it to his brothers, they hated him all the more" (NIV). Dreams and visions have been two of the ways God spoke in both the Old and the New Testaments to deliver messages and give direction and guidance to His people. God is still speaking through dreams and visions in our time.

Chapter 32

Hindrances to Prayer

Sin and Iniquities

We serve a faithful and compassionate Father who has promised that He will not withhold any good thing from them that walk upright (Psalms 84:11). Although He has given us promises, it behooves on us to walk in obedience to His Word because sin and iniquity will hinder our prayers and make it difficult or impossible for God to hear us. The prophet Isaiah said about the effect of sin: "But your iniquities have separated you from your God; your sins have hidden his face from you, so that he will not hear" (Isaiah 59:2 NIV).

King David knew the secret to receiving answers to his prayers. He lived a life of transparency by confessing instantly whenever he realized sin in his life. David committed the sin of adultery, murder, he was covetous, selfish, proud and greedy to name a few of them. However, when the prophet Nathan sent the Word of the Lord to him, he repented immediately. In Psalm 66:18 he said, "If I regard iniquity in my heart, the Lord will not hear me." Although David committed sins, he did not hide them in his heart but was repentant and confessed to God for forgiveness. David's example is worth emulating because if we confess our sins instantly any time we sin, we will develop a hatred for sin because sin brings fear, distress, steals our joy, brings panic and torment.

Any time the children of Israel sinned against God, they were defeated by their enemies. They had to repent and make confessions. Often times they fasted for restoration or made burnt offerings to God to atone for their sins. On other occasions the prophets of God interceded for them to be pardoned. The history of sin and its effects on the Israelites shows the necessity for us to rid ourselves of sin to receive answers to our prayers. In Joshua 7:11-13, God spoke through the prophet Isaiah saying:

> "Israel hath sinned, and they have also transgressed my covenant which I commanded them: for they have even taken of the accursed thing, and have also stolen, and dissembled also, and they have put it even among their own stuff. Therefore the children of Israel could not stand before their enemies, but turned their backs before their enemies, because they were accursed: neither will I be with you any more, except ye destroy the accursed from among you. Up, sanctify the people, and say, Sanctify yourselves against tomorrow: for thus saith the Lord God of Israel, There is an accursed thing in the midst of thee, O Israel: thou canst not stand before thine enemies, until ye take away the accursed thing from among you."

This was a clear message from the Lord that they will be defeated by their enemies because of the sin they had committed. The only way they could escape defeat was for them to repent and remove the sin from among them. There were no alternatives whatsoever. As people of God, we shall surely be defeated if we continue to walk in disobedience.

Unforgiveness is another weapon that the devil uses to hinder our prayers. In the Lord's Prayer, our Lord Jesus Christ taught us that we can only ask for forgiveness if we learn to forgive others their trespasses (Matthew 6:12). If there is unforgiveness in our hearts, then the enemy gains grounds to accuse us. The devil is the accuser of the brethren (Revelation

12:10). Discord and unforgiveness between spouses is another channel that the enemy uses to hinder our prayers (I Peter 3:7).

Wrong Motives

Wrong motives will also hinder our prayers. James 4:3 says, "When you ask, you do not receive, because you ask with wrong motives, that you may spend what you get on your pleasures" (NIV).

When God answers "No" to our prayer, it may not always be in His interest but we may be asking out of wrong motives such as greediness, envy, selfishness, pride and lust; that is why God will not hear us. For example, Haman desired and requested out of pride, selfishness and greediness which led to his destruction and all his household. Esther 6:6 says, "When Haman entered, the king asked him, 'What should be done for the man the king delights to honor?' Now Haman thought to himself, 'Who is there that the king would rather honor than me?'" (NIV). He asked for the king's royal apparel, the horse that the king rode and the crown the king wears all delivered by a noble prince. We should pray or desire with the right motives or out of a good conscience in order that our prayers will not be hindered.

Doubt

Another hindrance to our prayers is doubt. The Word of God declares in James 1:5-7 that, "If any of you lacks wisdom, he should ask God, who gives generously to all without finding fault, and it will be given to him. But when he asks, he must believe and not doubt, because he who doubts is like a wave of the sea, blown and tossed by the wind. That man should not think he will receive anything from the Lord" (NIV).

About nineteen years ago, I had an astonishing experience when I doubted God. It gave me a clear message about the negative consequences that doubt could lead us in our Christian walk.

I went to a dentist to have my premolar tooth extracted and because my gum was numbed by injection, I did not realize that the dentist was extracting my molar tooth instead of the premolar. When I became conscious of what had happened, my molar tooth had already been extracted. There was no need for argument because the harm had been done. On my way back home, I prayed a simple prayer out of my desperation. "Lord, you know the harm that has been done, but one thing I know is that you are able to restore my tooth."

When I got home that afternoon, I had a deep sleep. I did not bleed, neither did I have pain nor swelling. In my sleep I had a dream that someone appeared from the clouds and touched me. I cannot explain exactly what the person did to me, but the very next day, I saw a white tooth growing out of the place where the extraction was done. The growth continued and I shared the testimony with some brethren about what the Lord had done. I was scheduled to share my testimony at our next Full Gospel Business Men's Fellowship International meeting. Before then, the devil started throwing doubts into my mind. He whispered to me constantly, "The tooth you are seeing is a broken part of the extracted tooth that remained in the gum. Your gum is going to swell, because this is a dangerous thing." I was gripped with a terrible fear; therefore, I decided to go back to the hospital for an X-ray in order to investigate what was going on.

Before I ever had the opportunity to go for investigation, I dreamed again that a demon spirit with a dark appearance had entered my room presumably to make it impossible for me to figure out what that spirit was; but I knew that it was in the form of a human figure. I became dumb-founded. The very next day, I started having very severe pains in my left eye penetrating through the gum at the spot where the tooth was growing. To my astonishment, the tooth started growing backwards and vanished into my gum after a few days. That tooth has been covered by gum tissue until today.

I remember very well sharing this miracle with a colleague of mine who was a Biological Scientist. He happened to be one of the most brilliant and intelligent people I had ever met. He was inclined towards being a naturalist and did not show much interest in spiritual things. I offered him an invitation to the Full Gospel Business Men's Fellowship International Meeting where I was scheduled to share my testimony. He never asked any questions. He simply replied, "Percy, I will come." The opportunity never came for me to share the testimony. The devil stole the miracle by throwing doubts into my mind. I believe without any shadow of doubt that the testimony was going to bring this colleague of mine to Christ.

The devil opposed supernatural miracles during the time of the apostles, and he is doing the same today because he knows that it will cause people to believe in Jesus. John 12:10,11 says of Lazarus, "So the chief priests made plans to kill Lazarus as well, for on account of him many of the Jews were going over to Jesus and putting their faith in him" (NIV). The chief priests wanted to kill Lazarus in order to negate the miracle that Jesus had performed and to destroy the testimony in order to prevent people from believing in Jesus Christ.

When Peter saw Jesus walking on water, he had enough faith to also walk on water, but before long, he looked at the wind, waves and listened to the devil's suggestions which brought doubt and fear. Immediately he started to sink (Matthew 14:28-31). The devil is using the weapon of doubt to rob us of the miracles of God. He has succeeded in making people believe that God is no longer performing supernatural miracles in the name of Jesus. This notion is a fallacy. It is an orchestration of the devil. The miracles of Jesus and the Apostles are still available for us today if we would pray, fast and believe. For all things are possible to them that believe (Luke 1:37).

PART SEVEN
Prayer is the Key

Chapter 33

Seeing Through God's Eyes

*R*elationships take time and effort to develop, as does our relationship with God. It is imperative that we spend quality time and effort to pray on a more regular basis in order to develop a line of communication with God. Through our communication, God imparts His faith and understanding into our spirit and we begin to see through His eyes and see things the way He sees them. Our desires, ambitions, thought patterns and actions become Godly and His interests become our interests and His priorities our priorities.

Let us now ponder over some incidents in the Bible where people saw differently from what God was seeing and, thereby, understand and appreciate the need to keep on with the fellowship of God by communicating with Him and studying His Word.

Adam and Eve

When Adam and Eve were in fellowship with God, they were seeing through the eyes of God and did not see their nakedness until the devil deceived them to eat the forbidden fruit and sin against God. Genesis 2:16 says, "And the Lord God commanded the man, saying, Of every tree of the garden thou mayest freely eat; but of the tree of the knowledge of good and evil, thou shalt not eat of it: for in the day that thou eatest thereof thou shalt surely die." It is written of the devil in Genesis 3:4-5, "And the serpent said unto the woman, Ye shall not surely die: For God doth know that in the day ye eat thereof, then your eyes shall be opened, and ye shall be as gods, knowing good and evil." Adam and Eve did not need the help of the fruit to make them become like God because God had already made them in His image and likeness. It was a deceit of the enemy to destroy them or to separate them from God and make them into the image and likeness of the devil himself by lying to them that they would be like God.

> **Adam and Eve did not need the help of the fruit to make them become like God because God had already made them in His image and likeness.**

When they heeded to the deceit of the devil, Adam and Eve began to see through the eyes of the flesh and the eyes of the devil, and this made them realize their nakedness. Before their sin they were in a different state, were having an intimate fellowship with God and God was visiting them on a regular basis. When we continue to communicate with God on a regular basis, we tend to be bonded to Him which enables us to see through the eyes of God and for that matter the eyes of faith.

Moses and the Exodus

When Moses and the people of Israel got to the Red Sea and the Egyptians were chasing after them, God told Moses to go forward, but the Red Sea was before them and behind them was the Egyptian army. They complained bitterly to Moses about how he had brought them to the wilderness to perish. Someone may wonder what kind of a Father God is. After God had delivered them out of four hundred years of bondage with a strong-arm, signs and wonders and brought them thus far, how could they go forward seeing there was danger ahead. God being omnipotent, commanded Moses to stretch forth his rod on the sea, the water parted and the Israelites walked on dry ground. Exodus 14:15 says, "And the Lord said unto Moses, Wherefore criest thou unto me? speak unto the children of Israel, that they go forward."

When God was seeing dry ground before them, dead bodies, drowned horses and chariots of the Egyptian army behind, the Israelites were only seeing the Red Sea in front of them and the Egyptian army behind (Exodus 14:15). God being the Alpha and Omega knew what was ahead of them. God always finishes something before He starts. He knew the way He had already made for His people before He led them to the wilderness. Let us begin to understand the power of God which avails for us and see through the eyes of faith. We know without a doubt that the end of our salvation is finished on the cross. The end of your marital problems is finished on the cross. The end of your financial problems, job and whatever else is weighing you down has been rolled away on the cross.

Abraham and Sarah

God had given a promise to Abraham and Sarah that they would be fruitful and that their descendants would be as numerous as the stars in the heavens. After several years had passed and the promise had not been fulfilled, Abraham and his wife Sarah were discouraged.

Genesis 15:1,2 says, "After this, the word of the Lord came to Abram in a vision: 'Do not be afraid, Abram. I am your shield, your very great reward.' But Abram said, 'O Sovereign Lord, what can you give me since I remain childless and the one who will inherit my estate is Eliezer of Damascus?'" (NIV). "Then Abraham fell upon his face, and laughed, and said in his

233

heart, "Shall a child be born unto him that is an hundred years old? and shall Sarah, that is ninety years old, bear?" (Genesis 17:17). "Therefore Sarah laughed within herself, saying, After I am waxed old shall I have pleasure, my lord being old also? (Genesis 18:12).

Sarah had passed the age at which it was biologically possible for her to conceive and Abraham had grown weak in his body. In spite of their doubt, they had a son because God had spoken. While Abraham and Sarah were seeing old age, barrenness, the biological impossibilities, discouragement, disappointment and loss of hope, God was seeing fruitfulness, joy overflowing in their hearts, laughter, rejoicing, testimony and praise coming from their lips. God was seeing a table being prepared in the presence of their enemies and a multitude of descendants coming from them.

The Prophet Elisha and the Children of Israel

In the time of Elisha the prophet, there was severe famine in the land of Samaria to the point that mothers were slaughtering their children and eating them in order to survive. There were four lepers who sat at the gate of the city, and they reasoned among themselves saying, why do we sit here and die of this famine. If we go to the city we shall die. If we sit here we shall die. Therefore we shall go to the camp of the Arameans. If they spare us we shall live, if they kill us we shall die also (II Kings 7:3b,4). They eventually agreed to go to the camp of their enemies; and as they went forth in faith, God made their footsteps to sound in the ears of the Arameans as chariots and a mighty army. They said to one another, the Israelites have gone to hire the Hittites and the Egyptians to come against us (II Kings 7:6b). Therefore, they fled for their lives.

234

When the lepers arrived, they found an abundance of food and riches, and they shared this news with the Israelites who came to the camp in response to the news. The Israelites celebrated because of the abundance.

The women were looking at the natural and were slaughtering their children and eating them; what a devastating situation it was (II Kings 6:28,29). The prophet of God, Elisha, had prophesied concerning the deliverance of God from the famine but the king's officer doubted the prophet of God when he said that there was going to be abundance. He said, even if God opens up the floodgates of heaven this would not be possible (II Kings 7:2). The whole nation of Israel was seeing hunger, starvation and destruction; but God saw abundance because He knew how He was going to make the provision.

If believers would embrace and apply this principle and begin to see through the eyes of God and for that matter the eyes of faith, our lives would never be the same. Instead of walking in fear and defeat, we would see ourselves as conquerors and victorious people in Christ. Instead of seeing our problems, we would begin to see the solution to our problems. Instead of seeing sickness, we would see health and restoration. Instead of seeing a broken marriage, we would see a reunion, the return of a "lost" child and the deliverance of a loved one from substance abuse.

Whatever the need may be, let us continue to hope in God because hope will not make us ashamed. At any point in your life when all seems to work against you, remember the Psalmist's declaration, "Weeping may endure for a night, but joy cometh in the morning" (Psalm 30:5b).

Chapter 34

Garden of Eden Revisited

The Fall of Man

The devil knows that communication and fellowship with God is the key to spiritual and physical success. He works around the clock to destroy any form of communication and fellowship between us and God. He started this form of maneuvering in the Garden of Eden and has not relented. All the methods that were employed by the devil in the Garden of Eden are still being used by him today. His main objective was to break the fellowship between men and God and by so doing take the authority that God has given to men.

In the book of Genesis 1:26, it is written that God made man in His own image and likeness. He gave man the authority to rule over the fish of the sea and the birds of the air, over the livestock, over all the earth, and over all the creatures that move on the ground. God created man for fellowship with Him. He also said that it is not good that man should be alone, and, therefore, He made him a helpmate (Genesis 2:18). Man from the beginning radiated the glory of God and was given power and wisdom to name every thing that God had created. God had fellowship with Adam and Eve on a regular basis and they were in a godly state. But because they yielded to the devil's deceit, they were alienated from God and had to run from Him. Communication had broken down, they lost the authority, power, glory and dominion that they had from the beginning with God, because they heeded the devil's lies and ate the forbidden fruit.

They were translated from the Kingdom of Light to the Kingdom of Darkness.

The Great Messianic Prophecy

The fellowship between God and man was broken from then on. God had to find a remedy to restore man back to Himself because He loves us. He created us to love and fellowship with Him. In Genesis 3:15 God said to the serpent (Satan), "And I will put enmity between thee and the woman, and between thy seed and her seed; it shall bruise thy head, and thou shalt bruise his heel."

"This verse has long been recognized as the first messianic prophecy of the Bible. Thus, it also contains the first glimpse of the gospel. It reveals three essential truths: (1) that Satan is the enemy of the human race, explaining why God put enmity between Satan and the woman; (2) that He would place a spiritual barrier between thy seed (Satan's people) and her seed (God's people); and (3) that the representative seed of the woman (i.e., Christ) would deliver the death blow to Satan, but in so doing would be bruised Himself. "He shall bruise (crush) thy head, but thou shalt bruise his heel refers to Christ's bruising on the cross, which led to the eventual crushing of Satan and his kingdom.""

Hebrews 9:22 declares "And almost all things are by the law purged with blood; and without shedding of blood there is no remission." From the time of the prophecy to its fulfillment, blood of animals was used to atone for the sins of the people of Israel. The messianic prophecy was eventually fulfilled in the birth, death and resurrection of the Lord Jesus, in John 3:16 where it is written, "For God so loved the world, that he gave his only begotten Son, that whosoever believeth in him should not perish, but have everlasting life." God loved us so much that He had to pay the price to restore us back to Himself.

God's Covenant with Israel

God made a covenant with the children of Israel through Moses. In Exodus 24:7,8 we read, "Then he took the Book of the Covenant and read it to the people. They responded, 'We will do everything the Lord has said; we will obey.' Moses then took the blood, sprinkled it on the people and said, 'This is the blood of the covenant that the Lord has made with you in accordance with all these words'" (NIV).

The children of Israel were not able to obey the laws of the covenant because the Do's and Don'ts were too many for them to uphold, and sin continued to increase on the surface of the earth. The priests had to make animal sacrifices to cleanse themselves of their own sins and the sins of the people in order to restore them into fellowship with God, but unfortunately, the blood of bulls could not take away their sins permanently (Hebrews 10:4).

The Blood that Speaks

God made a provision to redeem man once and for all and to restore man to his former position of glory and fellowship with Him. In Hebrews 12:24 the Word of God declares, "to Jesus the mediator of a new covenant, and to the sprinkled blood that speaks a better word than the blood of Abel" (NIV). Through one man's (Adam) disobedience, sin and death came upon all humanity. By the death of Jesus Christ we have received forgiveness and restoration. He has paid the price for us (Romans 5:19). Hebrews 10:10 says, "By the which will we are sanctified through the offering of the body of Jesus Christ once for all."

We have been forgiven because of the blood. We are redeemed by the blood and we are restored by reason of the blood. We have been bought back by the blood of Christ and we have once again been translated from the Kingdom of Darkness to the Kingdom of Light. Jesus was a perfect sacrifice.

The revised version of "The Blood Will Never Lose Its Power" by the songwriter Andrae Crouch reads;

"The blood that Jesus shed for me
Way back on Calvary.
The blood that gives me strength from day to day.
It will never lose its power. It reaches to the highest mountain,
It flows to the lowest valley.
The blood that gives me strength from day to day.
It never lose its power."

We Have Power and Authority

Jesus has Taken Back the Power

Our faith, confidence, salvation, healing, deliverance, hope and all our victory are embodied in the death, burial and resurrection of our Lord Jesus Christ. In Revelation 5:12 it is written, "In a loud voice they sang: 'Worthy is the Lamb, who was slain, to receive power and wealth and wisdom and strength and honor and glory and praise!'" (NIV). Psalm 24:7-8 also declares, "Lift up your heads, O you gates; be lifted up, you ancient doors, that the King of glory may come in. Who is this King of glory? The Lord strong and mighty, the Lord mighty in battle" (NIV).

Jesus died, was buried, went into hell and took back the authority and power that had been taken away from man by Satan when Adam and Eve disobeyed. The gates of hell; the demons, principalities, powers and spiritual wickedness in high places were asking who the king of glory was because they thought Satan was the king of glory. Jesus defeated death and hell and took back the keys from the one who holds the keys of death and the grave, that is Satan. "Forasmuch then as the children are partakers of flesh and blood, he also himself likewise took part of the same; that through death he might destroy him that had the power of death, that is, the devil; And deliver them who through fear of death were all their lifetime subject to bondage" (Hebrews 2:14,15). Jesus has won the victory for you and me.

The writer of the book of Revelation testified about Jesus saying: "And when I saw him, I fell at his feet as dead. And he laid his right hand upon me, saying unto me, Fear not; I am the first and the last: I am he that liveth, and was dead; and, behold, I am alive for evermore, Amen; and have the keys of hell and of death" (Revelations 1:17,18). Jesus again declared, "All authority in heaven and on earth has been given to me. Therefore go and make disciples of all nations, baptizing them in the name of the Father and of the Son and of the Holy Spirit, and teaching them to obey everything I have commanded you. And surely I am with you always, to the very end of the age" (Matthew 28:18-20 NIV).

Jesus Walks with Us

Jesus, the one who has authority, is with us. He uses the authority on our behalf and this will be to the end of the ages. In Mark 16:17-18 it is written, "And these signs will accompany those who believe: In my name they will drive out demons; they will speak in new tongues; they will pick up snakes with their hands; and when they drink deadly poison, it will not hurt them at all; they will place their hands on sick people, and they will get well" (NIV). Jesus Christ is with us every moment as He had promised; when we call upon His name, we invoke His presence into our situation. It is He who performs all the miracles for us because He is with us.

> **When we call upon His name, we invoke His presence into our situation.**

We should begin to see ourselves and God as an earthly Father and his son. The son believes that his Father is strong, powerful and rich. Therefore, he runs to his Father in times of crisis or danger because he knows that the Father can fight all his "fights" for him. The child has no doubt whatsoever about the capabilities of his Father. We should have this childlike confidence in our dealings with God.

The Power is Restored

In Ephesians 4:8 the Apostle Paul wrote, "Wherefore he saith, When he ascended up on high, he led captivity captive, and gave gifts unto men." Jesus Christ has given gifts to believers to carry on His good works and to exercise the former dominion and authority that was taken away by the enemy in the Garden of Eden. Acts 1:8 says, "But you will receive power when the Holy Spirit comes on you; and you will be my witnesses in Jerusalem, and in all Judea and Samaria, and to the ends of the earth" (NIV). The Holy Spirit has been given to believers to carry out the great commission. We have the power and the gifts to carry out the mission that has been assigned to us. As Jesus told the disciples that as the Father has sent me so send I you (John 17:18). It is communication with God that will maintain and protect the power that is restored to us by the death and resurrection of Christ. The role and importance of our communication with the Lord, cannot be overemphasized.

The Same Old Serpent

Since Jesus has restored us into fellowship with God through the shedding of His blood, the devil who was with God before his fall (knowing that he has lost every form of redemption and salvation with its concomitant privileges) is working hard around the clock to get us separated from God, again and again through prayerlessness and disobedience. He does not want us to have fellowship with God and he makes a lot of suggestions that will take our minds off prayer.

Jesus asked in Matthew 26:40, "Could you men not keep watch with me for one hour?" (NIV). Jesus felt sorry for His disciples because they slumbered and slept instead of being alert and watching with Him in prayer. The devil knows that prayer has an inherent power to make us Godly and to gain many spiritual benefits. He always looks for opportunities to divert our attention and prevent us from praying.

In Genesis 3:5 the devil told Eve, "For God knows that when you eat of it your eyes will be opened, and you will be like God, knowing good and evil" (NIV). He was implying that he (the devil) wanted Eve to be like God her Father. The Word of God says in John 8:44b, "He was a murderer from the beginning, not holding to the truth, for there is no truth in him. When he lies, he speaks his native language, for he is a liar and the father of lies" (NIV). Do you think the devil wants you to be like God or Godly so that he would not have a place amongst us? He always says things that are opposed to the truth. He speaks lies freely without any shame or remorse because it is his nature. He never wanted Eve to be Godly neither did he want Adam and Eve to enjoy the position that he (the devil) had lost forever. He knew that when they ate the fruit they were going to be separated from God, and that is what he wanted to achieve. He was leading them into a trap that would alienate them completely from God.

The devil is the same old serpent, subtle and armed with lies and deceit. He knows that when we pray we will live Godly lives. Therefore, he makes prayer look burdensome. He hates prayer and hates to see anybody practice it. He makes it appear to be one of the most uncomfortable, difficult and unpleasant spiritual exercises in our Christian walk. If all believers were Godly, where would the devil's throne be?

The Devil Has an Agenda

Just as in the Garden of Eden episode, the devil whispers many things into our ears. He comes back again with the same old Garden of Eden deceit to break our fellowship with God. For instance, when you get home from work, he makes you feel that there is something more important to do when you decide to go before God in prayer even when it is your set prayer time. He begins his whisperings, "There is a TV program to watch." If you succeed in shutting off the TV, he will make someone call you on the phone. After the phone call, then a knock on your door. Then he reminds you of the drink in the refrigerator and that food. "Why don't you try it?" he tells you. "What about dry-cleaning?" "What about some shopping?" "What about that new CD?" "Why not listen to it, it was so good," he suggests. "After all you are tired, go to sleep, you can still pray in the morning."

If you were preparing to go to work he will tell you, "You are smart enough, you will succeed, you can make it without prayer." Then you say to yourself, "I will pray when I get back home." The cycle continues on and on until he defeats you. The devil's suggestions are more than can be recounted.

The devil is a liar, he is older and wiser than we are. He is smarter and more powerful than we are. He knows too well that the only way we can overcome him is to hook up to God through prayer, fasting and the study of His Word. Then we will be wiser, smarter and more powerful than he is because God imparts His anointing to us when we go before Him in prayer. The anointing breaks the yoke of sin and every bondage; which enables us to defeat the devil. This is the reason for the Prophet Isaiah prophesying, "And it shall come to pass in that day, that his burden shall be taken away from off thy shoulder, and his yoke from off thy neck, and the yoke shall be destroyed because of the anointing" (Isaiah 10:27).

The Devil Wants Us Dead Spiritually

All the weapons that the devil uses against us to prevent us from praying or talking to God prove that he wants to alienate or separate us from God. He meant the direct opposite of what he told Eve in the Garden of Eden. He knew that God had told them that the day they would eat of the fruit they would surely die (Genesis 2:17b). When they ate the fruit, they were separated from God; that is they died spiritually. The devil used this strategy right from the Garden of Eden and he has been using it until now. He wants us to be alienated from God or anything that is Godly so he will do everything in his power to make it difficult for us to pray or hearken to the voice of God. We should make prayer and the Word our priority because prayer is for our spiritual being as food is for our physical being. It is only through prayer that we can overcome sin and conquer the devil. He succeeded in alienating Adam and Eve from God through deceit. We also become alienated from God and we die spiritually when our spirit is starved through prayerlessness, a lack of fasting and the Word of God which are the food of the spirit.

As it does happen in marriage relationships whenever there is a communication breakdown between husband and wife, the marriage is falling on the rocks. When we don't pray consistently, it results in a communication breakdown and our relationship with God becomes sour and falls on the rocks, then we become "divorced" from Him.

The Rewards of Being Prayerful

A child of God who lives disorderly does not spend time in prayer, but a child of God who lives orderly and does the things of God spends time in prayer. As an illustration let us compare a child who lives with his or her parents and grows under their discipline to a street child. It is obvious that the street child will develop attributes that he has acquired from the street and may become a liability to society. The child who has learned discipline in the home will more likely be an asset to society because he or she has spent time with the parents and has acquired attributes from the parents.

This illustration explains why we need to spend time with God in order to develop Godly attributes. When we fellowship with God through prayer, we are able to walk in righteousness, holiness, in faith, and love. It is not us but God's spirit that lives His righteousness through us. Paul said in Galatians 2:20, "I am crucified with Christ: nevertheless I live; yet not I, but Christ liveth in me: and the life which I now live in the flesh I live by the faith of the Son of God, who loved me, and gave himself for me." The only way to overcome sin and live in holiness is to unite with God through prayer; it is the key to success in the spirit and in the natural because the devil only fears one who prays and is obedient to the Word of God.

As we continue to hear and receive from God, our lives are transformed and changed by the power and anointing behind His words; we speak the things He has communicated to us. We serve God with confidence, and we can stand firm in the face of adversity.

One of the rewards of prayer is that it produces Godliness which results in the fruits of the Spirit dwelling in us and helping us to overcome sin. Then the power of God begins to manifest in our lives as it was in the days of the apostles. When we speak the Word of God, it functions like God speaking it because of His creative ability in us. Jesus said, "I tell you the truth, anyone who has faith in me will do what I have been doing. He will do even greater things than these, because I am going to the Father" (John 14:12 NIV). He also promised in John 15:7, "If you remain in me and my words remain in you, ask whatever you wish, and it will be given you" (NIV).

These Scriptural verses are all pointers to the fact that we should first have intimacy with God through prayer. It is then, and only then, that as we remain in God, His words remain in us and we will do greater works as He has promised. Unfortunately, many of these verses have not been appropriately applied. We tend to focus on the greater works and receiving whatever we wish rather than remaining in God and His Words remaining in us. If we seek the kingdom and its righteousness, and walk in holiness, it is the blessing that will follow us rather than us chasing after blessings because the promise of God is yea and Amen.

NOTES:

PART EIGHT
Why Should We Fast?

Chapter 35

Why Should We Fast?

*B*efore I touch on the reasons why we should fast, I want us to first of all define fasting. According to the Webster's New World Dictionary, "fasting is to eat very little or nothing." The NIV also defines fasting as "to abstain from food, especially as a religious discipline." My definition of fasting is "to place the flesh under arrest," "to beat the flesh into submission," or further still, I would also describe fasting as "a heavenly remedy for earthly crises." My definitions are based on the revelation of the mystery of fasting which will unfold as we go along in this part of the book.

Jesus and the Apostles lived a life of fasting and left an example for us to follow. The purpose of fasting is manifold. It is to derive power for ministry, in decision-making or to be led by the spirit, for deliverance, healing, sorrow and repentance for sin. It is for humbling ourselves before the Lord, to walk in His presence and in confronting difficult spiritual battles. The Apostle Paul said he fasted often (II Corinthians 11:27). Jesus Christ told the disciples that when the bridegroom is taken away from them they would fast (Mark 2:20). He said about evil spirits in Matthew 17:21 "Howbeit this kind goeth not out but by prayer and fasting." God spoke to the children of Israel, "'Even now,' declares the Lord, 'return to me with all your heart, with fasting and weeping and mourning'" (Joel 2:12 NIV). There is a long list of Bible verses that admonish us to fast. We, as followers, are obligated to fast as part of our Christian walk and fasting is a command by God to be obeyed.

Power for Ministry

Before our Lord Jesus Christ started His ministry at the age of thirty, the Spirit of God led Him into the wilderness where He fasted and prayed for forty days and forty nights (Matthew 4:1). He received strength and power from God by fasting and praying. This power enabled Jesus to overcome all the temptations that the devil brought His way and defeated the devil.

In the Book of Acts we read that after the encounter of the Apostle Paul with the Lord on the way to Damascus, he went without food or drink for three days and immediately after this encounter he started preaching the Gospel. Acts 9:9,19a 20 says "And he was there three days without sight, and neither did eat nor drink...And when he had received meat, he was strengthened... And straightway he preached Christ in the synagogues, that he is the Son of God." I believe those three days of fasting prepared and equipped him for his journey in the ministry. Many people who have been called into ministry have testified that they waited on the Lord in prayer and fasting for God's direction and anointing in order to be effective.

Decision Making (to be led by the Spirit)

By fasting and praying we are empowered spiritually to help us in making our decisions. Jesus was God incarnate, but He prepared Himself for His ministry by waiting upon God for strength and direction. This initial preparation enabled Him to choose His Apostles. Jesus lived a life of fasting and prayer and did not do anything without first praying for guidance. Romans

8:14 says, "For as many as are led by the Spirit of God, they are the sons of God." "Trust in the Lord with all thine heart; and lean not unto thine own understanding. In all thy ways acknowledge him, and he shall direct thy paths" (Proverb 3:5,6). In choosing elders in the church, we should allow the Spirit of God to lead us. Many times we have looked on the outward appearance, level of education and one's wealth or status. In Acts 14:23 it is written, "And when they had ordained them elders in every church, and had prayed with fasting, they commended them to the Lord, on whom they believed."

As mentioned earlier, prayer and fasting help us to walk in the spirit and be led by the Spirit of God in our choices and decisions because the flesh is subdued as we pray and fast. Isaiah 58:11a says, "And the Lord shall guide thee continually..." Jesus, therefore, set an example for us to follow. In Luke 22:40, Jesus said to the disciples, "Pray that you will not fall into temptation" (NIV). We fall into many traps of the devil because we do not pray to seek God's direction. We are usually led by our thoughts, feelings, lusts and desires instead of being led by the Spirit of God, especially when it comes to issues of male-female relationships. Many people have perished or shortened their lives because of wrong decisions in the choice of life partners. In career choices, where to live and many other decisions in life, we need God's leadership in order to avoid the many troubles and temptations that we usually fall into.

Deliverance and Healing

Through fasting we receive healing from God for the diseases that afflict our bodies. In Isaiah 58:8 the prophet Isaiah prophesied thus, "Then your light will break forth like the dawn, and your healing will quickly appear; then your righteousness will go before you, and the glory of the Lord will be your rear guard" (NIV).

About thirteen years ago, I frequently had asthma attacks at night. I decided then to take some time off to fast before the Lord. On the fifth day of the fast, I dreamt that two extremely tall men had visited me and asked me to accompany them to my brother's place. On our way, one of the men thrust his fingers into my nostrils and removed something out of them. From that night in the Easter season of 1994 until now I have never had any symptoms of asthma. Praise be to His name. There is power in prayer and fasting. If we do not pray and fast, we will be robbing ourselves of blessings.

The results of prayer and fasting are awesome. I believe you too can be delivered from various forms of health issues such as paralysis, mental problems, cancer, sleeplessness, habits such as substance abuse, smoking and alcoholism which do not bring glory to God. If medication fails and prayer has not given you the breakthrough, add fasting to the prayer and Jesus says it will come out (Matthew 17:21) (more on this under "Confronting Difficult Battles").

> **If medication fails and prayer has not given you the breakthrough, add fasting to the prayer and Jesus says it will come out.**

God may not give you a dream as He did in my situation, but He will always meet our needs. To the blind man, Jesus put clay on his eyes. "And said unto him, Go, wash in the pool of Siloam..." (John 9:7a). To the leper He said, "Go show yourself to the priest" (Mark 1:42-44 NIV). To the woman who had an issue of blood He said, "Thy faith hath made thee whole" (Matthew 9:22). To the paralyzed man He said, "your sins are forgiven" (Mark 2:5b NIV). Jesus healed all manner of sicknesses (Matthew 4:23).

When we fast and pray, the body is taken out of the way and the spirit gains quick access to God's presence. Sickness and disease cannot withstand the presence of God and His anointing breaks the yoke of sickness (Isaiah 10:27). Sickness and disease have to automatically vanish from the presence of God (More on this under Unlocking the Mystery of Fasting). The healing which takes place in the spirit is then manifested in the body of the person. The Word of God declares that, "Surely he hath borne our griefs, and carried our sorrows: yet we did esteem him stricken, smitten of God, and afflicted. But he was wounded for our transgressions, he was bruised for our iniquities: the chastisement of our peace was upon him; and with his stripes we are healed" (Isaiah 53:4,5).

Sorrow and Repentance for Sin

Fasting was used by the Old Testament believers as a way of mourning and of repenting of their sins. God approved of it and demanded it of them when they erred from His statutes. "'Even now,' declares the Lord, 'return to me with all your heart, with fasting and weeping and mourning'" (Joel 2:12 NIV). We can apply this Old Testament principle when we err from God's statutes as a way of repentance and return to the Lord. Nehemiah 9:1,2 says, "Now in the twenty and fourth day of this month the children of Israel were assembled with fasting, and with sackclothes, and earth upon them. And the seed of Israel separated themselves from all strangers, and stood and confessed their sins, and the iniquities of their fathers."

Humbling Ourselves Before the Lord

Fasting enables us to empty ourselves of all egotistic or self-seeking tendencies and depend on God for help. It helps to humble us before the Lord. King David recalled that, "Yet when they were ill, I put on sackcloth and humbled myself with fasting"

(Psalm 35:13 NIV). The God of Israel also proclaimed, "if my people, who are called by my name, will humble themselves and pray and seek my face and turn from their wicked ways, then will I hear from heaven and will forgive their sin and will heal their land" (II Chronicles 7:14 NIV). Fasting is a means of humbling ourselves before God in prayer in order for Him to hear us.

Walking in His Presence

When Jesus Christ lived among the disciples, they did not need to fast because He was physically present with them. Jesus was the embodiment of all that the apostles needed because He was God incarnate. He told them that a time would come when He would be taken away from them, then they would fast. "They said to him, 'John's disciples often fast and pray, and so do the disciples of the Pharisees, but yours go on eating and drinking.' Jesus answered, 'Can you make the guests of the bridegroom fast while he is with them? But the time will come when the bridegroom will be taken from them; in those days they will fast'" (Luke 5:33-35 NIV). This passage suggests that since the Bridegroom (Jesus Christ) is not with us bodily, we have to fast often in order to subdue our flesh to be able to walk in the Spirit and live under His presence. Romans 8:8 says, "So then they that are in the flesh cannot please God."

When Prayer Does Not Produce Results

In the twentieth chapter of the book of Judges we read about an interesting account of the children of Israel and how fasting turned their defeat into victory. They had a dispute with the Benjamites and on two occasions they had prayed to God and asked council before going to battle. On both accounts they were defeated by the Benjamites.

When prayer alone has not produced results, we can use the weapon of fasting. After being defeated twice, the children of Israel decided to fast, pray, offered burnt offerings and peace offerings. This time they routed the Benjamites, smote and destroyed them. Judges 20:26,35 records, "Then all the children of Israel, and all the people, went up, and came unto the house of God, and wept, and sat there before the Lord, and fasted that day until even, and offered burnt offerings and peace offerings before the Lord...And the Lord smote Benjamin before Israel: and the children of Israel destroyed of the Benjamites that day twenty and five thousand and an hundred men: all those drew the sword." From this account we realize that they were able to defeat the enemy when they reinforced their prayers with fasting.

Confronting Difficult Battles

Jesus said, "Howbeit this kind goeth not out but by prayer and fasting" (Matthew 17:21). There are some problems that cannot be overcome until we fast and pray. This verse in Matthew's gospel affirms that there are different levels and ranks of evil spirits, some being more powerful than others. Unless we derive spiritual energy from God through fasting, it will be difficult for us to defeat some evil forces and overcome some strongholds in our lives.

This verse is so vital in our dealings with evil forces and it is interesting to know that it has been omitted in many versions of the Bible. It has been debated in some theological and Biblical arenas and some have agreed to omit it from many versions of the Bible with the reason that it is excluded or put as a footnote from the oldest manuscript. This reason does not add up. The devil knows very well that if we are able to pray, fast and study the Word, he can never defeat us because he was not able to defeat Jesus after He had fasted forty days in the gospel of Luke chapter four.

Right in front of me as I write, this verse has been footnoted in my New International Version; verse twenty (20) is followed immediately by verse twenty-two (22). Strange! Why? It was Jesus himself who made this statement when the disciples could not heal the boy with epilepsy. I thank God that there are still remnants of people who believe, and there are versions that have this verse.

Let us ask ourselves, "Why the struggle over this verse alone?" It is obvious that it is a direct and naked opposition of the forces of darkness. I believe there is no demon that cannot be overcome through prayer and fasting because Jesus never gave us any other option for dealing with evil forces. He did not give us other alternative steps to take if the demon does not go out after we have fasted and prayed. Therefore, prayer and fasting are the ultimate weapons which will annihilate all the forces of darkness which oppose us in our marriages, in our finances, on our job, strong holds in our families, in disobedient children, in addictions and in health issues.

> **Prayer and fasting are the ultimate weapons which will annihilate all the forces of darkness which oppose us.**

When medication has failed and you have laid hands on the sick without success, when the Elders have prayed over you and anointed you with oil, and all these have not brought solutions, prayer and fasting will produce results because of the mercy and grace we obtain. Hebrews 4:16 says, "Let us therefore come boldly unto the throne of grace, that we may obtain mercy, and find grace to help in time of need." There is divine power in prayer and fasting.

Charles and Frances Hunter said of Lee Bueno-Aguer: "Having received a death sentence from her doctors, Lee Bueno-Aguer has found that God has given her a better prescription-fasting to regain her health."

We will not allow anybody or the devil to deceive and rob us of our blessing that can only be obtained through fasting and prayer. God commanded that we should fast, Jesus Christ taught us to fast and great men of God have taught us to fast such as the Apostle Paul, Morris Cerullo, Derek Prince, Arthur Wallis, Gordon Lindsay, Benny Hinn and many, many more.

Derek Prince said, "On the basis of the record of the whole Bible, I would say that prayer and fasting combined constitute the strongest single weapon that has been committed to God's believing people. There is nothing more powerful than prayer and fasting available to the people of God. It is their greatest single weapon. If this is true, it is obvious that the devil will do everything in his power to keep people from recognizing and using this weapon."

We have to intensify and amplify the power of prayer through fasting in order to overcome those stubborn forces of darkness. Looking back at the context of the chapter, we find that Jesus Christ rebuked His disciples for having little faith (Matthew 17:20). Fasting and prayer, therefore, should increase our faith to overcome the forces of darkness by sharpening and improving our hearing capabilities, because faith comes by hearing and hearing by the Word of God (Romans 10:17).

Yokes of bondage such as sin and curses within a family, sicknesses, jobs, marital problems, educational problems, church problems and failure can be broken through prayer and fasting. The fasting and prayer should be intensified for greater spiritual energy to counteract all the forces that are behind a problem.

Matthew 11:12 says, "And from the days of John the Baptist until now the kingdom of heaven suffereth violence, and the violent take it by force."

We should take our victory by the force of prayer and fasting. National and international crisis can also be addressed by prayer and fasting. If we follow the history of the children of Israel, we would understand the role prayer and fasting played during their time of crisis. Whenever they were faced with a difficult situation, they proclaimed a fast and God intervened and brought deliverance. We too, have to confront the confrontations of the enemy by intensifying our spiritual energy and power through prayer and fasting.

> **We too, have to confront the confrontations of the enemy by intensifying our spiritual energy and power through prayer and fasting.**

Fasting is a Command

Jesus said to His disciples, "When you fast, do not look somber as the hypocrites do, for they disfigure their faces to show men they are fasting" (Matthew 6:16a NIV). Jesus in this statement was making an assumption that we would fast because we are His followers. He did not say "if we fast," which means that fasting was a must for His followers. Fasting should become part of our Christian experience in order for us to live victorious lives.

Fasting and prayer helps to draw us closer to God, and by so doing, we derive the spiritual energy to overcome obstacles in our way and to live Godly lives. Jesus, being God incarnate, brought His body under subjection and derived His strength from prayer and fasting. How much more should we who are the sons of men!

Chapter 36

When to Fast

*M*any times people have asked, "When should I fast?" The answer to this question is that the Bible has not given any calendar of fasting for Christians, however, periods of fasting both in the Old and New Testament have mostly been associated with difficult times. They fasted in times of danger, trouble, war, hardship, crisis, sickness, sin or in decision-making.

Times of fasting cannot be prescribed, but thanks be to God for the Apostle Paul for his letters to the Corinthians which gives us a clue to the question as to when we should fast. In II Corinthians 11:27, Paul confessed that he "fasted often." The phrase "fastings often" could not be interpreted as being a fast in the midst of crisis situation, sickness, war or any of the above reasons in the Old and New Testament for times of fasting. It could not be interpreted as fasting once in a year, neither is fasting often a daily practice or even a monthly observation. The Webster's New World College Dictionary defines "often" as "many times; repeatedly; frequently." From the context of the scripture, a good interpretation of the word "often" would be a weekly observation. Secondly, Paul did not confess that he fasted often because of a difficult situation meaning that fasting was part of his Christian responsibility just as prayer was.

261

Fasting often will help us keep our bodies under control, enable us to walk in the Spirit and bear the fruit of the Spirit. It will help us live in the anointing and equip us ahead of time to face difficulties or challenges. Like prayer, fasting is a must, it is obligatory for victorious Christian living. Evangelist Benny Hinn wrote, "I am convinced more than ever that fasting should be part of your normal Christian walk. It will strengthen your relationship with the Lord. The presence of God will become closer, and your prayer life will take on added power. Fasting in the name of the Lord Jesus will build a stronger, more potent faith. And fasting will intensify your prayer life."

In Matthew 6:7 Jesus said, "When ye pray...," and in Matthew 6:16, He said, "When ye fast..." which means that prayer and fasting is a must for believers. He did not say, "If you pray" or "If you fast" which would in that sense make prayer and fasting optional. With this clue in mind the number of days in the week and what day of the week to fast is left to each individual to decide as one is led by the Spirit and also depending on one's circumstances such as job and other commitments. Dr. Myles Munroe wrote, "Just as prayer is not an option for the believer, fasting is not an option. It is a natural expectation of God for His people."

In the Gospel of Luke 2:37, it is recorded, "And she was a widow of about fourscore and four years, which departed not from the temple, but served God with fastings and prayers night and day." Fasting was the lifestyle of Anna. She did not only fast when in need but as a spiritual service or responsibility to the Lord her God.

Once I was asked in a radio interview with Bob Dutko (WMUZ-FM 103.5, Detroit, Michigan): "Should one fast for a long time when he has a big problem and fast less when he has a small problem?" We take a clue for this question from Daniel's twenty-one day fast. In Daniel's account we are told that God answered his prayer the very first day of his fasting. However, the prince of Persia withstood the angel of God. It was not until Michael the Archangel came to help the angel, that the answer was released. Daniel prayed and fasted until he saw a breakthrough. Likewise, we should also battle in prayer and fasting until we experience a breakthrough and a victory no matter what kind of need, whether big or small. Here we see that Daniel's persistence in prayer and fasting brought him the victory. It behooves on us to also persevere in prayer and fasting whether our problems are small or big until we see our breakthrough.

How Long Should One Fast?

The number of days one fasts depends on the individual and on the leading of the Spirit of God. There is a record of different durations of fasting in the Bible:

a)   One night (Daniel 6:18)

b)   Till evening by the Israelites (Judges 20:26)

c)   One day (I Samuel 7:6)

d)   Three days and nights by Queen Esther and the Jewish community (Esther 4:16), Saul (Acts 9:9)

e)   Seven days (II Samuel 12:16-18)

f)   Ten days (Daniel 1:12)

g)   Fourteen Days by Apostle Paul (Acts 27:33)

h)   Twenty-one days by Daniel (Daniel 10:2,3)

i)   Forty days and nights by Moses, Elijah and
        Jesus Christ (Exodus 34:28; I Kings
        19:8, Matthew 4:1,2)

The durations listed are not prescriptions for fasting. It is up to the individual to fast as he or she is led by the Holy Spirit. However, we can follow these durations strictly if we so desire. Be it done unto you according to your faith.

Chapter 37

Unlocking the Mystery of Fasting –
Spiritual Benefits

*T*here are different forms of fasting recorded in the Bible, but fasting basically deprives the body of its nutrition, energy and satisfaction as already defined. The body is rendered weak through fasting and, therefore, cannot function as it normally does. The soul is also humbled and brought under subjection when we fast as was told by King David, "I humbled my soul with fasting" (Psalm 35:13b).

Enemies at War

In I Corinthians 15:44b it is written, "…There is a natural body, and there is a spiritual body." The natural body is visible but the spiritual body is not visible, and for that reason we usually overlook the spiritual body and nourish the natural body to the disadvantage of the spiritual body. We seem to pay more attention to the natural body to the detriment of the spiritual body.

Galatians 5:17 says, "For the flesh lusteth against the Spirit, and the Spirit against the flesh: and these are contrary the one to the other: so that ye cannot do the things that ye would." The NIV says, "For the sinful nature desires what is contrary to the Spirit, and the Spirit what is contrary to the sinful nature. They are in conflict with each other, so that you do not do what you want." In this verse we find two enemies in a battle, the flesh (the sinful nature) and the Spirit or the natural body and the spiritual body. Each of these is craving for our attention. These enemies are always contesting for supremacy, and whichever of the two that wins the battle, lords it over the defeated. The winner dictates to the defeated or makes decisions that please it. For this reason if we continue to neglect the spirit (spiritual body) and spend all our energies, time and effort to nourish and cherish the flesh (the natural body), the spiritual man becomes malnourished, lean and weak. Then the flesh becomes stronger, dictates and controls the spirit. What fasting does is, it focuses attention on the flesh and tries to beat it into submission in order for the spirit (the spiritual body) to overpower the flesh (the natural body).

Paul said to the Church in Rome, "There is therefore now no condemnation to them which are in Christ Jesus, who walk not after the flesh, but after the Spirit (Romans 8:1). This verse reveals that it is our responsibility to walk in the Spirit because Jesus has shed His blood to redeem us from condemnation. He has done His part and we also have our part to play by walking in the Spirit, for it is written, "they that are in the flesh cannot please God" (Romans 8:8). The way to walk in the Spirit is by bringing the body under control through fasting, prayer and the study of the Word of God.

Removing the Hindrance

Mr. Flesh vs. Mr. Spirit

Fasting is the means by which we are able to render the body ineffective or weak, then it becomes easier for its opponent (in this case the Spirit) to overpower, win the battle and rule over the body. The body (flesh) which stands in the way of the Spirit and has opposed it is taken out of the way of the Spirit. The Spirit is, therefore, liberated to live life to its maximum potential. As an analogy, let us consider two boxers in a ring: Mr. Flesh versus Mr. Spirit.

Mr. Flesh has an upper hand because of several advantages. For example, Mr. Flesh is well known and has a lot of support and as a result he has a psychological advantage over Mr. Spirit. Mr. Flesh is taller, heavier and has a longer reach than Mr. Spirit. He also has a physical advantage over Mr. Spirit; it is a complete mismatch.

The fight is also taking place in Mr. Flesh's home ground, which is the "World" and, therefore, the reason for his massive support and popularity. When the fight begins, it is apparent that Mr. Flesh will knockout Mr. Spirit, however, if we by any means succeed in tying Mr. Flesh's hands behind him and make it impossible for him to throw his heavy punches, then Mr. Spirit will get the upper hand and knock Mr. Flesh out.

Mr. Flesh vs. Mr. Spirit

Galatians 5:24-25 says, "And they that are Christ's have crucified the flesh with the affections and lusts. If we live in the Spirit, let us also walk in the Spirit." When we fast and deprive the body of its nutrition, energy and satisfaction, we tend to literally "tie the hands" of the flesh and render it ineffective in opposing, resisting or overpowering the Spirit. When the flesh is overpowered, then the Spirit becomes stronger, dictates and controls the activities of the flesh, that is when the fruits of the Spirit begin to manifest in one's life. It is of a necessity that we crucify the flesh in order to please God. For those of us that belong to Christ, the fasting prayer is a means of crucifying the flesh, with its pride, affections and the lusts of the eye. Romans 8:13 declares, "For if ye live after the flesh, ye shall die: but if ye through the Spirit do mortify the deeds of the body, ye shall live."

Access to God

In the absence of the flesh, which acts as a hindrance in the way of the Spirit, it is easier for the Spirit to relate much quicker to God or it becomes easier for the Spirit to enter the presence of God and to manifest the fruits and gifts of the Holy Spirit. Under this circumstance, the flesh is brought under subjection. The human being consists of a body, soul and spirit. Mr. Soul, a spectator at the ringside, humbled and afflicted by fasting identifies with Mr. Spirit the winner, unites with Him, and along they go. Psalm 35:13 says, "But as for me, when they were sick, my clothing was sackcloth: I humbled my soul with fasting; and my prayer returned into mine own bosom." When our flesh is ruling over our spirit, it will also rule over our soul, and that is when we walk in the flesh and fulfill the lusts of the flesh.

I read a tract which talked about 32 spiritual and 32 physical benefits of fasting. One of the benefits was that fasting is the speediest method known to "spiritual power." From the foregoing, it is very clear that the speed with which fasting attains "spiritual power" is a result of the flesh which acts as the hindrance being taken out of the way of the Spirit. In God's presence we derive spiritual energy and power from God to help us overcome. Hence, the anointing and power which God imparts to the spirit is also transferred automatically to the body and the body manifests it in healing and faith. The fruits and the gifts of the Spirit are also demonstrated in one's life. This means that fasting changes us and puts us in a position to obtain mercy and receive answers from God.

The shadow of the Apostles healed the sick. The touch of Jesus' garment healed the sick. Aprons which had touched the Apostles healed the sick, therefore, gaining access to the "shadow," the presence and a touch of God by prayer and fasting will certainly heal us of any infirmity. Herein lies the secret as to why fasting has spiritual benefits. The power of God rests on us and we will do the work of the ministry under the power of the Holy Spirit.

> **Gaining access to the "shadow," the presence and a touch of God by prayer and fasting will certainly heal us of any infirmity.**

Dave Williams wrote, "A pastor friend of mine discovered one day that he had cancer and was going to die. It was a heart-breaking discovery, especially since he didn't want to leave his church, and the church didn't want him to leave. One of the elders of the church went before the congregation and said, 'Pastor's got cancer. The doctors say he's going to die. We can't afford to lose him. We need to fast.' The church fasted on behalf of their pastor, and within a week the cancer was gone. My friend went on for many more years as pastor of that church. Fasting brought a miracle of healing!"

Oh! What a testimony. The benefits of prayer and fasting are awesome and we cannot comprehend the whole mystery. It is time for the church of God to wake up from our sleep and slumber. This is the time for spiritual awakening for a revival in the body of Christ for the manifestation of the power of God in our midst. There is a need for the church to go back to their roots from where the apostles started and the need of that cannot be over emphasized:

> Mark 16:15-18,20 says, "And he said unto them, Go ye into all the world, and preach the gospel to every creature. He that believeth and is baptized shall be saved; but he that believeth not shall be damned. And these signs shall follow them that believe; In my name shall they cast out devils; they shall speak with new tongues; They shall take up serpents; and if they drink any deadly thing, it shall not hurt them; they shall lay hands on the sick, and they shall recover...And they went forth, and preached every where, the Lord working with them, and confirming the word with signs following. Amen."

Earthly Flesh

"The spirit indeed is willing, but the flesh is weak" (Matthew 26:41b). This passage of Scripture reveals that the flesh is easily misled; it is quick to compromise. It is easy to fall victim to sin and earthly desires because it was made from the earth. The flesh is easy to fall into temptation as the verse implies. Therefore, we need to bring it

> **The flesh is easily misled; it is quick to compromise. It is easy to fall victim to sin and earthly desires because it was made from the earth.**

270

under the subjection of the Spirit through prayer and fasting.

The flesh unites with our enemies to fight against us because it does not want to fast neither does it want to pray because these are exercises which feed the spirit and not the flesh. We have to place the flesh under check in order that it may not mislead us.

The flesh always wants to be destructive; it wants to taste, hear, see, feel, smell, say something, touch, do this or that, go here or there, be angry, strive, fight, argue, lie, curse and feel proud. It is egotistical. Therefore, fasting is a means of "shutting up" the flesh and its weaknesses so that our spirit can become sensitive and receptive to God and be in control. We should bear in mind that the flesh will never ever do the things of God because it is earthly. The Spirit in us should always be strengthened by prayer, fasting and the Word of God in order that it will be able to put the flesh under check at all times. Paul said in I Corinthians 9:27, "But I keep under my body, and bring it into subjection: lest that by any means, when I have preached to others, I myself should be a castaway."

I have learned over the years that we all have to bring our bodies under the subjection of the Spirit - Preachers, Teachers, Pastors, Prophets, Evangelists and all Christians - because it is one thing to preach or teach and another thing to implement the Word because it is our individual responsibility. We all have to work out our own salvation with fear and trembling. As a matter of fact, Christian leaders are at a greater risk because the Scripture tells us to whom much is given, much is required. Jesus was addressing people in leadership when He spoke saying, "Many will say to me in that day, Lord, Lord, have we not prophesied in thy name? and in thy name have cast out devils? and in thy name done many wonderful works? And then will I profess unto them, I never knew you: depart from me, ye that work iniquity"

271

(Matthew 7:22-23).

Jesus and the apostles understood this principle and they disciplined themselves through prayer and fasting. If the flesh is left alone, it will always do things that are contrary to the things of the Spirit, and we cannot please God.

What is the Difference?

The Human Being was made from a combination of the flesh (from dust) and the Spirit (from God). Since the flesh (body) was made from the dust of the earth, it is fed with food, it is dependent on food which is grown from the dust, and because the flesh is from the dust of the earth, it does things that are earthly and contrary to the Spirit. As the Bible says in Romans 8:8, "So then they that are in the flesh cannot please God."

Our Spirit is from God. "The Lord God formed the man from the dust of the ground and breathed into his nostrils the breath of life (our spirit), and the man became a living being" (Genesis 2:7 NIV). Our spirit can survive and get strong if we feed it with the things of the spirit such as prayer, fasting, and the Word of God. Jesus said, "It is written: 'Man does not live on bread alone, but on every word that comes from the mouth of God'" (Matthew 4:4 NIV). We should give more attention to the spirit because the body which was made from dust does not have much value since it is the spirit that gives life to the body (dust). When we die, the body is good for nothing no matter how much attention and money we may decide to give and spend on the body (remember the story of the "Four Boyfriends" from chapter two).

It is interesting to know that when we die the body is separated from the spirit and goes back into the dust and the spirit returns to God from where it came. God proclaimed in

Genesis 3:19 that, "By the sweat of your brow you will eat your food until you return to the ground, since from it you were taken; for dust you are and to dust you will return" (NIV).

> We have to strengthen our spirit through God's Word, prayer and fasting. These are the foods of the spirit which give spiritual nourishment, energy and vitality to the spirit just as food provides nourishment, energy and vitality to the body.

In order for one to be able to walk in the Spirit as the Word of God commands us, we have to strengthen our spirit through God's Word, prayer and fasting. These are the foods of the spirit which give spiritual nourishment, energy and vitality to the spirit just as food provides nourishment, energy and vitality to the body.

Chapter 38

Unlocking the Mystery of Fasting – Physical Benefits

*P*eople do get positive results from fasting even though they may not be Christians. The reason for this positive result is that fasting does not have only spiritual but also physical benefits. Physiologically the immune system functions twenty-four hours daily to fight foreign or unwelcome organisms and substances that enter the body especially through food. Microorganisms such as fungi, protists, bacteria, viruses and toxic substances (such as pesticides, drugs, and other toxins from fertilizers) and pollutants that enter the body are destroyed by the immune system.

The body falls sick when these unwelcomed substances overpower the immune system or when the activities of the unwanted substances overshadow the immune system.

In the absence of the regular supply of food during times of fasting, the immune system directs its activities on the "other" foreign substances in the body. It identifies organisms causing infections in the skin and body, boils, pimples and other foreign deposits like excess cholesterol are destroyed by the immune system. Cancerous cells which are all "foreign" to the body are also destroyed by the immune system. Daniel 1:15 says, "And at the end of ten days their countenances appeared fairer and fatter in flesh than all the children which did eat the portion of the king's meat." In spite of the fact that Daniel and his friends fasted on vegetables and water, they were fairer because of the combined effects of the spiritual and physical benefits of fasting in their body, soul and spirit.

Dave Williams in his book, The Miracle Results of Fasting said, "Hippocrates, the father of modern medicine, saw fasting as the remedy within," and he quoted Hippocrates as saying, "Everyone has a doctor in him or her, and we just have to help it in its work. The natural healing force within each one of us is the greatest force in getting well. Our food should be our medicine; our medicine should be our food but to eat when you're sick is to feed your sickness."

Dave Williams said of Hippocrates, "In other words, he recognized that our bodies are wired to fight sickness. He went on to say that 'if we are sick, it can be made worse if we keep feeding the sickness without a pause, and that pause is fasting."

By fasting, we are starving the disease-causing organisms; we are allowing the immune system to fight the organisms, and we are blocking the supply of nutrients to the foreign or cancerous cells. With increased and intensified spiritual energy, the anointing breaks the yoke of sickness. Here we find the effects of both spiritual and physical forces combining to effect a healing or restoration process in the physical body.

Dave Williams quotes Dr. Otto Buchinger as saying that, "Fasting is, without any doubt, the most effective biological method of treatment." He calls it 'the operation without surgery' because it re-attunes, relaxes, and purifies our systems."

Usually at the end of every long fast, the digestive system is purged and cleansed of every waste or toxic substance which confirms Dr. Buchinger's claim that fasting purifies our system.

The Mysteries of Prayer and Fasting Tied Up

Now that the mysteries in Prayer and Fasting have been unlocked, we have a better insight as to why these weapons are so powerful and effective.

Fasting removes the flesh which acts as a hindrance that stands in the way of the Spirit. With the hindrance removed, there is a quick entry or access to the throne-room of God, and by prayer we invoke the presence of God into our lives. This produces Godliness, faith, anointing, wisdom, knowledge, power, creativity and other attributes which we derive from God and results in a release of the supernatural abilities of God into our lives. With the presence of God manifested so mightily upon us, sin and iniquity cannot rule us; sickness and disease cannot survive in our bodies; principalities and demons cannot resist our power; doubt cannot interfere in our faith; wrong motives cannot intrude our minds; and the victory becomes ours.

I would conclude with a mathematical equation in an attempt to summarize the mysteries:

If A is directly proportional to T, then $A = kT$ where

A = Anointing
(God's presence in one's life)

T = Time spent
(in prayer and fasting)

k = Constant
(prayer and fasting)

$$A = kT + O$$
Where
A = Anointing
k = Prayer and Fasting
T = Time Spent
O = Obedience

Obedience to the Word of God is a prerequisite for God's anointing upon one's life, but with exceptions to the rule, the final equation becomes:

$$A = kT + O, \text{ where } O = \text{Obedience to God's Word.}$$

The anointing or presence of God on an individual's life is dependent upon the amount of time one spends in fasting and communicating with God and the level of understanding, acceptance and obedience to the Word of God. Elizabeth George, author of A Women After God's Own Heart wrote, "The impact of your ministry to people will be in direct proportion to the time you spend with God. We want our strength in public to be explained by what goes on in private between us and God."

We should bear in mind that for every analogy, there is some limitation; this mathematical illustration is no exception and it is not without limitation. For example, the time spent plays an important role but the quality of the communication is of equal importance.

There is a deeper mystery to the subject of fasting than we can ever imagine. Let us think of it; what kind of parent will make their children go on a hungry stomach before they respond to their need? No one! Over the years, I have come to experience and believe that there is more divine power in prayer and fasting than we have ever or will ever know. As a matter of fact we cannot explain the "whole" mystery. There is a hidden mystery that is only known to God. Deuteronomy 29:29 says, "The secret things belong unto the Lord our God: but those things which are revealed belong unto us and to our children for ever, that we may do all the words of this law." The secret things belong to God. I believe fasting is one of the secret things that belongs to God. The bottom line of the whole matter is that there is power in fasting and prayer.

On the basis of my personal experience, from biblical accounts and the testimonies of others, I would conclude that, there is no gainsaying that fasting is God's remedy, antidote, a heavenly medication to the sick, solution to man's earthly problems and leads to a greater anointing in the ministry. We cannot explain the whole mystery of fasting.

There is no gainsaying that fasting is God's remedy, antidote, a heavenly medication to the sick, solution to man's earthly problems and leads to a greater anointing in the ministry.

Chapter 39

Types of Fasting

*T*here are different types of fasting that were practiced by God's people which enabled them to defeat the enemy and do many exploits. All the fastings that were done both in the Old and New Testaments such as, Moses' fast, Elijah's fast, Samuel's fast, Hannah's fast, Cornelius' fast, Joel's fast, David's fast, Daniel's fast, Nehemiah's fast, Ezra's fast, Esther's fast, Jesus' fast, John the Baptist's fast, Anna's fast (widow's fast), Paul's fast and all other fasts can be categorized into five kinds of fasts and these are assigned different names in different circles. The duration of the fast may differ but basically all these fasts fall into one of five categories.

Supernatural Fast

Physiologically man can live without water for only about three days, because water forms approximately eighty percent of the total body weight. The body needs water for all the vital metabolic processes to go on successfully, and since the Supernatural Fast is without eating or drinking water, it has to be divinely directed by God without which there could be destruction instead of victory.

In Exodus 34:27, 28 it is recorded, "Then the Lord said to Moses, 'Write down these words, for in accordance with these words I have made a covenant with you and with Israel.' Moses was there with the Lord forty days and forty nights without eating bread or drinking water. And he wrote on the tablets the words of the covenant - the Ten Commandments" (NIV).

God called Moses to receive the covenant He made with the children of Israel on Mount Sinai. The divine presence of God made it possible for him to survive the forty days of fasting. After the fast, the Glory of God radiated from his face so much that the people of Israel were unable to look upon his face.

Jesus Christ was led by the Spirit to the wilderness to fast for forty days and forty nights before He started His ministry. Like Moses before him and Jesus after him, Elijah also fasted forty days and forty nights. All supernatural fasts in the Bible lasted for forty days and nights.

Total Fast

The Total Fast is also done without eating any food or drinking water. The difference, however, is that it is done for short periods. Usually it should not exceed three days because if the body does not get a supply of water after three days, it may lead to dehydration and a disaster. This fast is very effective for those who are able to practice it.

The world system is structured in such a way that it is very difficult for many people to go on a Total Fast. There is so much constraint due to commitment to work, family and other life concerns. The devil has made it almost impossible for people to go on a total fast. He does not want anyone to be Godly; therefore, he makes many commitments in "his world" to prevent people from fasting.

We have to be determined to win the war against the enemy by finding time to fast and pray. For those who cannot do the total fast there are other types of fasts that are equally helpful. In Esther 4:16 we read that Queen Esther declared a fast of three days and nights without food or water. In the book of Acts 9:9 Paul also fasted three days after the Lord appeared to him on his way to Damascus. This type of fast is sometimes referred to as the Absolute Fast or Dry Fast.

Non-Total Fast

The Bible describes two kinds of fasts that was done by Daniel. The first was with only vegetables (Non-Total Fast) and the second was with no pleasant bread (White Fast).

The Non-Total Fast is done by drinking water, eating vegetables and taking some fruit or fruit juices such as orange, pineapple, grape or a fruit that one may find convenient. It is believed in some circles that Jesus went on this type of fast because He was hungry after the forty days and nights but not thirsty, suggesting that He might have drunk some water or some fruit juices.

This type of fasting enables one to have enough energy to do battle with the enemy. Much of the weaknesses that are experienced during a Total Fast are avoided and so are the discomforts. The Total Fast is more effective for the one who is able to carry it through, but for those who cannot do it due to the many daily commitments, the Non-Total fast is equally helpful to pray through obstacles which can only be overcome through fasting. Daniel and his three friends went on this type of fast (Daniel 1:12).

White Fast

In Daniel 10:3 we read, "I ate no pleasant bread, neither came flesh nor wine in my mouth, neither did I anoint myself at all, till three whole weeks were fulfilled." The type of bread which Daniel ate is not very clear but the objective of fasting is to "crucify" the flesh by depriving it of anything that stimulates it. Some people have gone on this type of fasting by only eating carbohydrates such as bread, potatoes, rice or any starchy foods without salt or sugar and with no delicacies or spices.

Ordinary Fast

This is the most common type of fasting that has been practiced by many people. It is very convenient and much easier to carry out than the other types described above. It is usually done from midnight till six p.m. Judges 20:26 says, "Then the Israelites, all the people, went up to Bethel, and there they sat weeping before the Lord. They fasted that day until evening and presented burnt offerings and fellowship offerings to the Lord" (NIV). David and his men mourned and fasted until evening when they heard of Saul and Jonathan's death (II Samuel 1:12).

Some people end the ordinary fast at three p.m. or at noon depending on their age, the condition of the body such as pregnancy or other health conditions and also because it is easier to accommodate. Be it done unto you according to your faith (Matthew 9:29). The Ordinary Fast could be done as a Total Fast (without water), a Non-Total Fast (with water and fruit juices) or a White Fast (without delicacies) depending on how one chooses to do it, but it is for very short durations (few hours) as already indicated. It can also be done for several days depending on how one is led by the Holy Spirit.

Many working people have found this kind of fasting to be very helpful. The essence of fasting is not to starve the body but to get closer to God by subduing the flesh. Any approach that suits an individual could be done to obtain positive results. The Ordinary Fast is also classified as a Normal Fast.

> **The essence of fasting is not to starve the body but to get closer to God by subduing the flesh.**

Misconceptions About Fasting

Fasting from T.V., Shopping and other Pleasures

Many people have bought into the concept of fasting from T.V., from shopping and other kinds of fasting. Taking a close look at the definition of fasting and also from the Biblical point of view will reveal the real meaning of fasting. The NIV defines fasting as "abstaining from food especially as a religious discipline." Webster's Dictionary also defines fasting as "to eat very little or nothing."

Fasting is also a conscious determination to abstain from food or to regulate the intake of food for religious purposes. For example, if you have not made up your mind or purposed in your heart to fast and for some reason you have not eaten because you did not have time, you cannot call it a fast or turn your starvation into a fast.

From the above definitions it is apparent that any other type of activity which does not abstain from food or does not exclude food cannot be identified as fasting. To explain this further, the Prophet Isaiah in chapter fifty-eight of his book explained that while you are fasting, meaning, when you are abstaining from food as a religious discipline, you should stay away from pleasures (e.g. T.V., shopping, movies, etc.) in order for you to be able to focus your attention on God. The time spent on T.V. and shopping should rather be spent communing with God, studying His Word or reading an inspirational book. Therefore, if you are not fasting or abstaining from food, staying away or ridding yourself from watching T.V. or shopping cannot be considered as a fast as long as it does not involve abstaining from food. Jentezen Franklin said in his book on fasting, "When you fast, you abstain from food for spiritual purposes. I have heard people say that they were planning to fast TV or computer games or surfing the Internet. It is good to put those things down for a time of consecration if they are interfering with your prayer life or with your study of God's Word or your ministering to the needs of others, but technically, that is not fasting."

Truly speaking, people do not want to pay the price any more, therefore, we are looking for an easy way out of spiritual discipline and sacrifice. We are looking for a "drive through and microwave" kind of spirituality so we are trying very hard to introduce our own concepts into scripture. In other words there is no Biblical basis for today's ideas of fasting only from T.V. or fasting from shopping, phone, surfing the internet, etc.

Let us ask ourselves: "What of someone who lives in a rural area, for example in a third world country who does not have a T.V. or does not have money for shopping? Would this person ever fast in his or her life since he or she does not have a T.V? Would we imply that the person has been fasting all through his or her life because he or she has never watched T.V?" This does not add up. It is understandable that one is abstaining from the pleasure of watching T.V. or that the one who does not have T.V. can also deprive himself or herself from something that he or she gets pleasure from, but as long as the person is not abstaining from eating food or regulating the food intake, the meaning of, or condition for fasting is not being fulfilled. Therefore, none of these abstinences can be considered as fasting.

We have to go back to the old-time religion of "sackcloth and ashes" which is a symbol of seriousness or mourning. The flesh loves food because they are from the same "mother" which is the earth. If you compromise or give the flesh a chance, it will never allow you to fast. It will give you false concepts, theories and philosophies that will give it the liberty to eat and eat its way to spiritual bankruptcy and decline.

> **If you compromise or give the flesh a chance, it will never allow you to fast. It will give you false concepts, theories and philosophies that will give it the liberty to eat and eat its way to spiritual bankruptcy and decline.**

Dr. Myles Munroe writing on fasting said, "Fasting is intentional abstinence from eating…In the Old Testament, the Hebrew word for fast is tsum. It means 'to cover over the mouth.' In the New Testament, the Greek word is nesteuo. It means 'to abstain from food.' A fast is a conscious, intentional decision to abstain for a time from the pleasure of eating in order to gain vital spiritual benefits."

Let us have a word of caution here so that people will not take this too extreme. There is nothing wrong with fasting and watching a T.V. program of a revival meeting, a teaching from Scripture, preaching or even listening to the news on world events which could lead you to intercede. What we need is to apply wisdom and be selective in what we do during times of fasting. What Isaiah is saying here is that there is time for everything. When we are on a fast, we should abstain from deriving pleasure or trying to satisfy the flesh which contradicts the Spirit and does not afflict the soul (Isaiah 58:3). The Apostle Paul gave us one good example on some of the pleasures between a husband and a wife. I Corinthians 7:5 says, "Defraud ye not one the other, except it be with consent for a time, that ye may give yourselves to fasting and prayer; and come together again, that Satan tempt you not for your incontinency."

Can I Fast when I am Sick and on Medication?

People have asked questions like: "Can I fast when I am on medication? Can I fast when I have high blood pressure, diabetes or an ulcer?"

In the beginning of this part on fasting I described fasting as "a heavenly remedy for earthly crises." The mystery of fasting is deeper than we can ever comprehend. God is so omniscient (all knowing) and so omnipotent (all powerful) even more than we can ever know or imagine. Only God knows why He said we should fast as His beloved children or go on an empty stomach when we are in dire need of His help. It seems irrational to our earthly minds. Heavenly principles as a matter of fact are almost always irrational to the human mind. It is in this that the power of God is manifested in our lives. In I Corinthians 1:18 it is written, "The preaching of the cross is to them that perish foolishness; but unto us which are saved it is the power of God." God knew from the beginning that people will be on medication, He knew that people will have high blood pressure and He knew that people will have diabetes and other diseases. Oh, don't tell me that God did not know that people will have ulcers.

Drs. George and Hazel Hill wrote, "I have personally attested to, experienced and seen amazing results during and after a Daniel fast. I have seen people with stomach problems totally healed, ulcers disappear, and blood disorders healed. I have even heard of people getting back their natural hair color."

What did the prophet Isaiah say? "Is not this the fast that I have chosen? to loose the bands of wickedness, to undo the heavy burdens, and to let the oppressed go free, and that ye break every yoke?...Then shall thy light break forth as the morning, and thine health shall spring forth speedily: and thy righteousness shall go before thee; the glory of the Lord shall be thy rearward" (Isaiah 58:6,8). To this end it becomes a question of faith in Jesus Christ. For this reason the Son of Man came. In Luke 4:18 it is written, "The Spirit of the Lord is upon me, because he hath anointed me to preach the gospel to the poor; he hath sent me to heal the brokenhearted, to preach deliverance to the captives, and recovering of sight to the blind, to set at liberty them that are bruised."

If you believe you shall see the glory of God, therefore, be it done unto you according to your faith. If you believe, you will be healed of high blood pressure, diabetes or ulcers through fasting according to the prophet Isaiah. Your healing and deliverance from ulcers, high blood pressure and diabetes will spring forth speedily (Isaiah 58:8). The prophet went on to say, "But he was wounded for our transgressions, he was bruised for our iniquities: the chastisement of our peace was upon him; and with his stripes we are healed" (Isaiah 53:5).

Gum and Mint

Now to the big question of "Gum and Mint." This could be a very controversial issue so I want to address this subject from a biological point of view in order to make it understandable.

Whenever we consume a bowl of food, the food is first of all digested, part is converted to waste and eliminated from the bowels and the remainder is converted into sugar, amino acids, fatty acids and glycerol which are absorbed into the blood stream. These provide us with energy and the required ingredients of the body. The proportion of assimilated food depends on the type of food eaten. When we chew gum and eat mint, all the sugar in the gum and mint is absorbed directly into the blood.

You thought you were only chewing gum and eating mint to keep you from bad breath, but you are assimilating a lot of sugar directly into your blood. You are assimilating almost the same amount of sugar just as anyone consuming a regular meal if you ate about a handful of mint.

From the above analysis it is obvious that we are feeding our bodies when we chew gum and eat mint, just like any person who is eating or consuming food. Therefore, we do not satisfy the condition of a fast which is to abstain from food or regulate the intake of food when we eat and chew mint throughout the day of our fast.

Our focus should be to do what is pleasing to God and not to avoid the so called "offensive odor" or "bad breath."

Chapter 40

Beginning a Fast

As we practice fasting, we become more acquainted with its involvements and, thereby, know what suits our bodies best. However, I will offer a few suggestions that may be helpful when beginning a fast:

- Pray that God will give you the grace, strength and determination to carry the fasting through.

- Start by getting into the fast gradually. For instance, when undertaking a Total Fast, you may start off with an Ordinary Fast for the first day, a Non-Total Fast on the second day and then continue through with the Total Fast for the three day period.

- One may also go into a Total Fast by starting off with the Non-Total Fast or White Fasting for a day or two and then continue with the Total Fast for three days. Likewise, one can enter into the Non-Total fast by starting off with the Ordinary Fast.

The Last Fruit and Vegetable Meal

I had read from Arthur Wallis' book, 'Gods Chosen Fast,' which said, "Some advocate having fresh fruit only on the last day before fasting, that is if the fast is to be for a number of days." He went on to say that "Dr. Buchinger, who advocates this, suggests that the "fruit day" ensures that the last meal left in the bowel is fruit, which is less putrefactive than other food residues."

I was almost in the middle of a three-week non-total fast when I felt that I should visit the restroom only to realize that I had severe constipation. When I tried to push down on my bowels, I sensed without any doubt that I did not have the energy to do so.

As I tried harder to push on my bowels, I felt dizzy and lost almost all the energy left in me and immediately the Spirit of God led me to stop pushing on my bowels, otherwise, I could be in serious danger. All of a sudden I felt very weak and almost blacked out. I then got out of the restroom and ran to the kitchen to get some fruit juice in order to gain some energy. From there I went to lay flat on the floor and started sweating all over. I knew then that if I had insisted on bearing down on my bowels, I would have passed out and that would have led to disaster or even death.

It was then that I remembered what I had read some years back with regards to the last vegetable or fresh fruit meal before a long fast. The feces were as hard as stone and only heaven knows how I managed to get the hard stuff out. It took me about four hours of rest, prayer, taking some grape juice to restore energy and some effort on my part to get the hard stuff out of my bowels. I believe God wanted me to share this experience in order for people to understand how important it is to apply knowledge in times of a long fast. The last vegetable or fruit meal with its fiber will prevent such constipation so in the event of having to visit the restroom during a fast, one will have free bowels and will not encounter any problems.

Obstacles to Fasting

During times of fasting, you may experience less breakthrough because the devil will try to resist every attempt to be defeated. He will launch attacks from all directions. Discomfort is one of his weapons and sicknesses become more intense during times of fasting. The devil revisits his Garden of Eden ploys. He makes fasting a very difficult practice, and because of this some people have relegated fasting or made it a thing of the past. One of the natural reactions of the body is to feel sick when it is deprived of the normal supply of food it is used to. Sometimes you tend to feel like someone who has been bed-ridden with sickness. Your mouth feels bitter, and it is during those times that you experience what the Psalmist described as the affliction of the soul.

In 1994, when I was healed and delivered from asthma attacks, I knew at the time that my end was near during the fast because I had never experienced the effects of the disease as intense as I felt at that time. Little did I know that my deliverance was just around the corner. There is a saying that, "it always gets darkest before it is dawn." Make a determination to win the battle at these times and continue until you win the victory. Endure the suffering to the end knowing that the benefits of the fast far outweigh the suffering.

Arthur Wallis said, "Do not make the mistake of judging the efficacy of your 'battle' by what you feel. Quite often in seasons of prayer and fasting you will find the going tougher instead of easier and will seem to experience less rather than more liberty. This is often when most is happening. This is wrestling, it is heavenly warfare."

When the spiritual energy is intensified, that is when you will feel the strongest opposition from the forces of darkness. They will try to unleash their last straw to cause you to give up the fight when their defeat is near. This is the time that one experiences "the last kicks of a dying horse." Remember the epileptic in Mark 9:20a,26a, "When the spirit saw Jesus, it immediately threw the boy into a convulsion...The spirit shrieked, convulsed him violently and came out" (NIV). When the anointing on Jesus was too great for the demon to survive, it "kicked" very hard in an effort to destroy because its end was near. A similar thing happens when the anointing is increased by fasting. Victory through prayer and fasting is real and the benefits are awesome. Don't give it up.

> **When the spiritual energy is intensified, that is when you will feel the strongest opposition from the forces of darkness.**

I went on a seven day fast to seek the Lord on some issues. At the end of the fast, I had an encounter with the forces of darkness. One of the issues I had prayed about was for the healing of a pain. The pain was no better at the end of the fast, and I had a terrible feeling of discouragement, disappointment, hopelessness and I even felt suicidal (in the sense that life was not worth living; a feeling I had never experienced before).

The frustration persisted for about a day, and then God came on the scene. My discouragement turned into encouragement, disappointment turned into appointment with God, hopelessness turned into hope and a very strong faith that I would receive answers from God. The suicidal feeling turned into joy of living, and I started experiencing a breakthrough.

It looks like by going on the seven days of fasting, drinking only water, I had "slapped" the devil in the face and he literally slapped me back before surrendering. His "slap" was the discouragement, disappointment, hopelessness and suicidal feeling that I experienced.

In a nutshell, fasting is like telling the devil: "you will not rule my life," "I will not live a defeated life but a victorious life," "I will not live a sick person but live healthy," "I will not walk in unrighteousness" or that "I will live in obedience to God's Word."

I hope this experience will encourage someone who might have a similar encounter with the forces of darkness to let you know how the devil gives his last "kicks." He does everything to remove even the thought of fasting from our minds. Whenever you feel defeated after a fast, know that you are on the road to your breakthrough!

Many people have not been able to fast because the devil intimidates them with fear of dizziness, sickness, deep hunger and severe discomforts. It is during times of fasting that food smells and tastes best. The devil makes you feel that you have not eaten for days, only when you decide to fast. All these are the efforts of the enemy to make fasting impossible for many believers. These suggestions are the same old tricks he used in the Garden of Eden to deceive Adam and Eve. It is the devil's intention to separate believers from God and prevent them from receiving their full blessings from God through fasting. When one is able to resist these suggestions, the devil leaves them for a season. In my personal experience with fasting, the period that I grew physically strong and energetic was when I embarked on a Non-Total fast for fourteen days on water only. If one is able to stand against the suggestions and deceptions of the devil, all the dizziness and hunger dies out, but we should always remember that he will come back again when you are almost on the verge of getting a breakthrough with "the last kicks of a dying horse."

Ending a Fast

The actual process of fasting may not be as difficult as breaking the fast. This is the time that one needs a lot of restraint. There is always a temptation to eat a lot, to make up for the fasted food. A lot of self-control is needed at this time because eating too much could lead to disastrous consequences when breaking a long fast.

The Ordinary Fast can be ended very easily without any harm. Light food or fruits may be eaten, then a complete meal could follow later on without any damage to the bowels. Likewise the White Fast can also be ended with ease. The Total Fast and Non-Total Fast, however, should be ended with much precaution.

Biology of Fasting

Biologically, three important things happen to the digestive organs and the body during a prolonged fast:

1.   The stomach gets smaller and smaller as the fasting proceeds and a little amount of food at the end of the fast makes one full too soon because the stomach looses its original capacity.

2.   The digestive organs enter into a kind of "hibernation" with almost no activity at all. Therefore, like a newborn baby's digestive system, one should be very cautious of what enters the system. Liquids should be used to set

the stomach into a gradual activity until days later when normal foods are introduced. A lot of discipline and self-control are required at this time.

3.   The body and for that matter the digestive organs do not have the energy to digest and assimilate the normal quantities of food that it is used to digesting. This is because the stomach has been deprived of its source of energy for a long time. That is the reason why it is necessary to start off with juices which do not need too much energy for churning. The Total Fast will take more days to end than the Non-Total Fast. When the body is ready for heavy food, it should be taken a little at a time.

Arthur Wallis said, "It is of utmost importance that the food be eaten slowly, and so masticated that it is reduced to liquid before swallowing. At the first sensation of fullness in the stomach you should stop, even if you haven't completed your portion. Discomfort following a meal should be regarded as a signal to ease off and, if necessary, miss the next meal. This is where self-discipline is needed."

Attitude in Fasting

In Isaiah 58, the attitude that is expected of us during fasting is outlined:

•   We should avoid engaging in pleasure and involvement in other secular activities.

•   We should neither strive nor debate, and we

must refrain from wickedness.

• We should do good and show love to others.

• We should honor God and control our tongue.

• It is required of us to walk in righteousness and obedience to God, then will our light break forth as the morning and our health shall spring forth speedily.

Jesus Christ spoke against hypocrisy in fasting. Fasting, like prayers, should be done in secret (Matthew 6:6). The Pharisees were very much interested in the praise of men rather than glorifying God. They did their praying (fasting) in a hypocritical manner in order to be seen by men and their praying (fasting) was not pleasing to God. Like the Pharisees of old, some people are in the habit of broadcasting that they are undergoing a fast. It ought not to be so, however, much depends on the motive for telling others about your fast. For instance Jesus taught that:

"When you fast, do not look somber as the hypocrites do, for they disfigure their faces to show men they are fasting. I tell you the truth, they have received their reward in full. But when you fast, put oil on your head and wash your face, so that it will not be obvious to men that you are fasting, but only to your Father, who is unseen; and your Father, who sees what is done in secret, will reward you" (Matthew 6:16-18 NIV).

If we develop the habit of wanting others to know that we are in a fast, then we will be undertaking a fruitless fast like the Pharisees. As much as possible, we should keep our fasting to ourselves so that our fast will be unto God and not unto men in order that we will have a full reward from God. However, it is the intent of the one fasting that matters, because we cannot always keep our fasting to ourselves in some circumstances.

Fasting Turns Tide Around

There is an incredible account in the Book of Esther which reveals what could be accomplished as we fast and pray. King Nebuchadnezer took the Jews captive and carried them away to Babylon. Among the Jews was a man named Mordecai who brought his uncle's daughter by the name of Esther with him. She had lost both of her biological parents and was parented by Mordecai. Esther was a beautiful woman, who later became the Queen of King Ahazeurus who reigned in Babylon and many other provinces.

A man named Haman in Ahazeurus' kingdom was promoted above all the princes in the land. Haman planned to lay hands on Mordecai and all the Jews because Mordecai refused to bow and make reverence to him. Haman promised to pay ten thousand talents of silver to the King's treasury in order for the Jews to be destroyed. When the news reached Mordecai, he rent his clothes, put on ashes and cried bitterly. He then sent a message to Queen Esther about Haman's plot. Queen Esther declared a fast among all the Jews and her maids. Her intention was to approach the King with a petition on behalf of Mordecai and the Jews because it was against the law to go before the King when you had not been called.

Esther, through intercession, obtained favor in the eyes of King Ahazeurus. God intervened in their situation and turned the tide around. In the end Haman and all his household were hanged on the same gallows that he had prepared for Mordecai. What makes this whole episode outstanding is that they only fasted to be delivered from destruction by Haman, but they experienced many breakthroughs that they had not prayed about. The following account from the book of Esther chapter two through nine tells the story of the wonderful things that God did for the Jews as a result of their three days of fasting and prayer.

In the Book of Esther 6:1, it is written: "On that night could not the king sleep, and he commanded to bring the book of records of the chronicles; and they were read before the king." The king found out from the book of Chronicles that Mordecai had saved his life from an assassination plot by Bigthana and Teresh.

King Ahazeurus requested of Haman the kind of reward to be appropriate for the one the King delighted to honor. Then Haman thought in his heart, "To whom would the King delight to do honor more than myself?" (Esther 6:6b). Haman gave a long list of rewards because he thought that he would be the one to be honored. The one to honored turned out to be Mordecai to the bewilderment of Haman, so Mordecai was arrayed by Haman according to his own recommendations to the King.

Esther 6:12b,13 says, "...But Haman hasted to his house mourning, and having his head covered. And Haman told Zeresh his wife and all his friends every thing that had befallen him. Then said his wise men and Zeresh his wife unto him, If Mordecai be of the seed of the Jews, before whom thou hast begun to fall, thou shalt not prevail against him, but shalt surely fall before him."

Haman was hanged on the same gallows that he had prepared for Mordecai. King Ahazeurus then gave Haman's house to Esther and Haman's ring to Mordecai. And it came to pass that the Jews had joy and gladness and many of the people of the land became Jews for the fear of the Jews fell upon them (Esther 8:17). Esther also requested that Haman's ten sons be hanged on the gallows which Haman himself had built and it was done (Esther 9:14).

Esther 10:3 says, "For Mordecai the Jew was next unto king Ahazueras, and great among the Jews, and accepted of the multitude of his brethren, seeking the wealth of his people, and speaking peace to all his seed." In all of this we see the power of God being demonstrated in the lives of God's people as a result of prayer and fasting.

NOTES:

PART NINE
Recipients of a Blessing

Chapter 41

Recipients of Blessing

The Bible is replete with examples of God-fearing people who were obedient to Him, and through their obedience obtained blessings of a very high level. The Apostle Paul said, "I press toward the mark for the prize of the high calling of God in Christ Jesus" (Philippians 3:14). Paul revealed in this verse that God is calling us to a higher level of blessing. He is calling us to a higher spiritual and material blessing.

There are so many verses in the Bible which speak of the willingness and readiness of God to bless His people, but unfortunately, many Christians have lived below their potential until death. I will now take you through a line of characters in the Bible to examine how they applied the Word of God and the role obedience through prayer and fasting played to help them in their accomplishment of a higher blessing.

Obedience was the key to the success of the many people who obtained the higher blessing, and they could not be obedient to God without prayer and fasting. They had a personal relationship with God who gave them the enablement to live righteous and holy lives. There was what I call the "Forsaking Element" in their lives. They had to forsake "something" in order to obtain "another."

Robert Coleman wrote, "There had to be a complete forsaking of sin. The old thought patterns, habits, and pleasures of the world had to be conformed to the new disciplines of the kingdom of God."

Abraham and the Promise of a Nation

All nations of the earth have been blessed through the seed of Abraham, that is Jesus Christ our Lord and Savior. The Bible calls Abraham a friend of God because of his faithfulness (James 2:23). Friendship only develops when people communicate. Abraham could not have been a friend of God without communicating with Him, which made it possible for him to be influenced by God's Spirit and character that enabled him to obey God in faith and absolute trust.

> **Friendship only develops when people communicate.**

Abraham was blessed by God because of his obedience and he became the founder of the Jewish nation (Genesis 12:1-4). God tested Abraham's faith and obedience; He said to him, "Take your son, your only son, Isaac, whom you love, and go to the region of Moriah. Sacrifice him there as a burnt offering on one of the mountains I will tell you about" (Genesis 22:2 NIV). Abraham obeyed God and did according to what God had directed; he never questioned God about offering up Isaac as a sacrifice. He had trust and confidence in God because he had walked with Him and knew whom he had believed.

For many years Abraham waited for Isaac, his son of promise and after Isaac was born he was ready to offer him as a sacrifice in spite of the fact that he was his only son of promise. He loved God more than his son of promise and turned his back on Isaac. Not only did Abraham love God more than Isaac, but he also turned his back on his father's idols when he left his homeland for the promised land because it was not pleasing to God and God, therefore, pronounced a blessing upon him saying:

> "I swear by myself, declares the Lord, that because you have done this and have not withheld your son, your only son, I will surely bless you and make your descendants as numerous as the stars in the sky and as the sand on the seashore. Your descendants will take possession of the cities of their enemies, and through your offspring all nations on earth will be blessed, because you have obeyed me" (Genesis 22:16-18 NIV).

Joseph the Dreamer

The life story of Joseph is an epitome of consistent obedience to the Lord. His obedience is exemplary and worthy of emulation. Potiphar's wife cast her eyes upon him and said to him daily, "lie with me." It was an opportunity for Joseph to take advantage of his master's wife because he would have received the best of treatment in the palace, but Joseph feared God and had purposed in his heart to obey the Lord and not to sin against Him. Joseph communicated with God and God communicated with him through dreams most of the time. He couldn't have known God and been obedient to Him without a relationship existing between him and God.

Let us read Joseph's response when Potiphar's wife made sexual advances toward him; he said to her, "No one is greater in this house than I am. My master has withheld nothing from me except you, because you are his wife. How then could I do such a wicked thing and sin against God?" (Genesis 39:9 NIV). Joseph was a Godly person and highly favored. He did not see himself as sinning against Potiphar but against God. Due to frustration and shame, Potiphar's wife laid a charge against Joseph which resulted in his incarceration.

"The Lord was with him; he showed him kindness and granted him favor in the eyes of the prison warden. So the warden put Joseph in charge of all those held in the prison, and he was made responsible for all that was done there. The warden paid no attention to anything under Joseph's care, because the Lord was with Joseph and gave him success in whatever he did" (Genesis 39:21-23 NIV). The prison keeper committed all the prisoners into the hand of Joseph because he saw that the Lord was with him. He was faithful and trustworthy in whatever his hands found to do. God gave to Joseph the gift to interpret dreams and by that gift the Lord eventually brought him out of prison, blessed him and raised him to a very high position in the land of Egypt where God used him to save the Israelites during the seven years of famine. He was exalted because he humbled himself and was obedient to God in all things. Joseph was not boastful or full of pride but gave all glory to God.

Moses and the Ten Commandments

Moses fasted for forty days and forty nights to receive the Ten Commandments of God. At the end of the fast, his face radiated the glory of God to the point that the people of Israel could not look upon his face when he returned from the presence of the Lord. Through Moses' fasting and communication with God, he received an anointing which enabled him to perform supernatural acts.

The Bible says that Moses was the humblest person who has ever lived on the face of this earth (Numbers 12:3). Moses was of Jewish descent but was raised up in Pharaoh's palace in the land of Egypt and had the throne of Egypt within his reach. He was favored by Pharaoh because he was a Godly person.

In spite of all the earthly blessings within his reach, he forsook the idols of Egypt with all their riches, the throne with all its fame which he was supposed to inherit and chose to suffer with his people for the sake of the God of Israel (Hebrews 11:24,25). Because Moses was such an upright person, God raised him highly and delivered the people of Israel through his hands. Moses spoke face to face with God and God wrought mighty miracles through him. Through the hand of Moses, God brought plagues upon the people of Egypt which caused Pharaoh to free the children of Israel from slavery. Exodus 14:21,22 says, "Then Moses stretched out his hand over the sea, and all that night the Lord drove the sea back with a strong east wind and turned it into dry land. The waters were divided, and the Israelites went through the sea on dry ground, with a wall of water on their right and on their left" (NIV). Communication and fasting was the key to Moses' greatness and success.

Elijah the Great Prophet

"So he got up and ate and drank. Strengthened by that food, he traveled forty days and forty nights until he reached Horeb, the mountain of God" (I Kings 19:8 NIV). Elijah practiced fasting and he received a special anointing and blessing from God. He was taken up to heaven without experiencing death. II Kings 2:11,12 says:

"As they were walking along and talking together, suddenly a chariot of fire and horses of fire appeared and separated the two of them, and Elijah went up to heaven in a whirlwind. Elisha saw this and cried out, 'My father! My father! The chariots and horsemen of Israel!' And Elisha saw him no more. Then he took hold of his own clothes and tore them apart" (NIV).

During Jesus' transfiguration, Moses and Elijah appeared. Moses represented the Law, Elijah represented the Prophets and Jesus represented the New Testament. These were the three men of the Bible who fasted forty days and forty nights. Fasting and prayer definitely had a role to play in the achievements of these great men of God:

- They were all transfigured (Matthew 17:2,3).

- Moses parted the Red Sea (Exodus 14:21,22); Elijah parted the Jordan river (II Kings 2:6-8); and Jesus walked on water (Mark 6:49,50).

- No man saw the dead body of Moses (Deuteronomy 34:1-6); Elijah was taken up without seeing death (II Kings 2:11,12); and Jesus was taken up into heaven after His resurrection (Luke 24:51).

- Moses called Manna from heaven for the Israelites (Exodus 16:4); Elijah multiplied food for the widow and her son (I Kings 17: 12-16); and Jesus multiplied food for five thousand men (Matthew 14:19,20).

Moses, Elijah and Jesus performed supernatural miracles. Oh! What a parallel the lives of these men portray as a result of prayer and fasting. If believers would catch the vision of the power and potency of prayer and fasting, we would begin to experience the fullness of the potential God has placed in us, and we would likewise obtain and experience the highest form of the blessings that God wants us to enjoy.

Ruth and Naomi

Ruth was a Moabite who married Naomi's son Mahlon during the sojourning of Naomi's family in the land of Moab because there was famine in Bethlehem. It came to pass that Elimelech, Naomi's husband died and her two sons Mahlon and Chilion also died. Naomi then urged her daughters-in-law, Ruth and Orpah, to return to their native lands. Ruth, however, opted to follow Naomi, her mother-in-law, back to Bethlehem after the famine was over, but Orpah returned to her land and the gods of her people.

Ruth left her people and their gods and chose to serve the God of Israel. She cleaved to Naomi and vowed that only death could separate them. Naomi had no choice but to return to Bethlehem with Ruth her daughter-in-law. While in Bethlehem, Ruth found favor in the eyes of Boaz a wealthy man who was Elimelech's kinsman. Boaz took Ruth as his wife and she gave birth to Obed. Obed gave birth to Jesse, Jesse gave birth to David and Jesus Christ was of the seed of David.

Jesus was of the lineage of Ruth a Moabitess, a foreigner and an idol worshipper, but she was blessed because of her obedience and service to the God of Israel and to Naomi. She forsook idolatry and her own people to serve the living God of Israel. How blessed we would be if we could forsake our idols and serve the living God. Idol worshipping could come in various forms some of which may not be obvious, but anything such as people worship, love of money, pride of life, education and other "gods" which take first place in our lives instead of God is idolatrous. I believe Ruth could not have been that prosperous without communicating with the God of her mother-in-law and for that matter the God of Israel.

Jesus Christ and Human Salvation

The Apostle Paul writing to the Philippians about the Lord Jesus Christ said:

"Who, being in very nature God, did not consider equality with God something to be grasped, but made himself nothing, taking the very nature of a servant, being made in human likeness. And being found in appearance as a man, he humbled himself and became obedient to death - even death on a cross! Therefore God exalted him to the highest place and gave him the name that is above every name, that at the name of Jesus every knee should bow, in heaven and on earth and under the earth, and every tongue confess that Jesus Christ is Lord, to the glory of God the Father" (Philippians 2:6-11 NIV).

Jesus Christ did nothing without first praying to God (John 8:28). He fasted forty days and nights and obtained the spiritual strength that helped Him to defeat the devil in the wilderness. Prayer and fasting was His lifestyle and He received power and anointing which made it possible for Him to be able to humble Himself and obey God.

Jesus emptied Himself of His deity, His rightful position and was obedient unto death. God, therefore, exalted Him and gave Him the highest position because of His humility and obedience.

Paul the Great Apostle

Paul lived a life of fasting and prayer. He is one of the most powerful of the apostles ever recorded in history. He wrote thirteen epistles which have brought manifold spiritual and material blessings to the body of Christ. "God did extraordinary miracles through Paul, so that even handkerchiefs and aprons that had touched him were taken to the sick, and their illnesses were cured and evil spirits left them" (Acts 19:11,12 NIV).

Paul the great apostle lived an exemplary life. For the sake of the gospel he chose not to marry, he sacrificed his life and suffered many things for Christ's sake. In his letter to the Corinthians he said:

"Of the Jews five times received I forty stripes save one. Thrice was I beaten with rods, once was I stoned, thrice I suffered shipwreck, a night and a day I have been in the deep; in journeying often, in perils of waters, in perils of robbers, in perils by mine own countrymen, in perils by the heathen, in perils in the city, in perils in the wilderness, in perils in the sea, in perils among false brethren; in weariness and painfulness, in watching often, in hunger and thirst, in fastings often, in cold and nakedness" (II Corinthians 11:24-27).

Paul was totally sold out for the gospel and his sacrifice was rewarded. There is no apostle, preacher or pastor who has been able to confidently say that we should learn from them or learn their way of life since they are of Christ who agrees with what they teach (I Corinthians 4:17). At the final stage of his life Paul said, "I have fought a good fight, I have finished my course, I have kept the faith: Henceforth there is laid up for me a crown of righteousness, which the Lord, the righteous judge, shall give me at that day: and not to me only, but unto all them also that love his appearing" (II Timothy 4:7,8). Paul said he fasted often, and we all know that a fasting apostle must have been a prayer warrior. The importance of fasting and prayer cannot be over emphasized in our Christian life.

Abraham forsook his own son Isaac and chose to sacrifice him to God because God had demanded this of him (Genesis 22:1, 2). Joseph forsook adultery with Potiphar's wife and chose to suffer affliction in prison rather than to sin against God (Genesis 39:7-9). Moses forsook the riches and the idols of Egypt and chose to suffer affliction with the people of Israel. "By faith Moses, when he had grown up, refused to be known as the son of Pharaoh's daughter. He chose to be mistreated along with the people of God rather than to enjoy the pleasures of sin for a short time" (Hebrews 11:24,25 NIV). Ruth forsook the idols of Moab and chose to follow Naomi to serve the God of Israel (Ruth 1:15,16). Jesus Christ forsook His position and emptied himself of His deity to take upon Himself the form of man (Philippians 2:5-7). Paul forsook his personal comforts and sold his life out for the spreading of the gospel that has brought life to many people.

Let us be imitators of Jesus Christ, the captain of our salvation and empty ourselves of unrighteousness in all its forms. Let us trust that God will exalt us and give us the higher blessing that He has purposed for us. We should humble ourselves and forsake fornication and adultery as Joseph did. Like Moses, let us not trust in uncertain riches. Like Abraham and Ruth, let us forsake idolatry in all forms - people worship, materialism, money, education, egotism, pride and the many other idols that can take the place of God in our lives unknowingly. Like Elijah, let us walk with and serve the Lord. The God of Israel who was with these men and women of old will be with us and bless us richly with all spiritual and material blessings. Like Paul, let us fight the good fight of faith knowing that there is a crown awaiting us which the righteous judge will give us on that final day.

The scripture says, "The night is far spent, the day is at hand: let us therefore cast off the works of darkness, and let us put on the armor of light. Let us walk honestly, as in the day; not in rioting and drunkenness, not in chambering and wantonness, not in strife and envying. But put ye on the Lord Jesus Christ, and make not provision for the flesh, to fulfill the lusts thereof" (Romans 13:12-14). "Wherefore seeing we also are compassed about with so great a cloud of witnesses, let us lay aside every weight, and the sin which doth so easily beset us, and let us run with patience the race that is set before us, Looking unto Jesus the author and finisher of our faith; who for the joy that was set before him endured the cross, despising the shame, and is set down at the right hand of the throne of God" (Hebrews 12:1,2).

Let us not forget that we can rise to these levels, receive the higher blessings and realize our dreams by drawing nigh to God through prayer, fasting and obedience to His Word which are the keys to our breakthroughs both in the spirit and in the natural.

Chapter 42

What Next?

*A*fter you have done all that you know to do; you have done all that you have been taught to do; and all that you could and can and still have no results; all hope is gone, and your faith has been threatened with a question in your mind, "Does God really answer prayer?"...What do you do next? Many people have said, "I have fasted and prayed for a long time and nothing has happened, what else should I do? The natural thing that you may do is to put on an attitude, withdraw from church, prayer and Bible study. Jesus' answer to you is, "Don't give up." Continue to trust God, continue to fast and pray and do whatever you have been told to do by the Lord.

Jesus knew that we would experience such frustrations and discouragements but He has a Word for you, "And he spake a parable unto them to this end, that men ought always to pray, and not to faint" (Luke 18:1) and the NIV version says, "Then Jesus told his disciples a parable to show them that they should always pray and not give up." Let us read another parable by Jesus from Luke 11:5-10:

> "And he said unto them, Which of you shall have a friend, and shall go unto him at midnight, and say unto him, Friend, lend me three loaves; For a friend of mine in his journey is come to me, and I have nothing

to set before him? And he from within shall answer and say, Trouble me not; the door is now shut, and my children are with me in bed; I cannot rise and give thee. I say unto you, Though he will not rise and give him, because he is his friend, yet because of his importunity he will rise and give him as many as he needeth. And I say unto you, Ask, and it shall be given you; seek, and ye shall find; knock, and it shall be opened unto you. For every one that asketh receiveth; and he that seeketh findeth; and to him that knocketh it shall be opened."

In the book of Daniel 10:12,13, Daniel persevered in prayer until he received an answer to his prayer. Little did he know that God had already answered his prayer the very first day he purposed in his heart to seek God, but it was being delayed by the Prince of Persia. If Daniel had given up on God, he would not have received his answer. Zechariah and Elizabeth did not know that God had answered their prayer, but it was to be fulfilled in their old age (Luke 1:13).

Like Daniel, have you considered that probably God has answered your prayer and found the right spouse for you, but the enemy is trying hard to stand in the way of your breakthrough? Do you know whether God has opened a door of opportunity for you to get the job you are seeking? Your application may probably be in line waiting for you to be called. Do you know whether God healed you of your infirmity in the spirit but it is only to be manifested in the physical? Do not give up, continue to ask, seek and knock. Like Daniel continue to persevere in prayer and fasting and you will have your breakthrough whatever it may be.

In the gospel of Luke, Peter and his brethren had toiled all night without any success at catching fish, but Simon told Jesus "...nevertheless at thy word I will let down the net" (Luke 5:5b).

You may have prayed all night, you have prayed for months and years without any result. Like Simon Peter, confess that you will nevertheless launch into the deep. You will not give up, you will press on, you will hold on till you see your breakthrough. You will continue to trust God and seek and you will find.

Has God spoken to you? Has he given you His promise through His Word, through a dream or by prophecy? Habakkuk 2:2,3 says, "And the Lord answered me and said, Write the vision, and make it plain upon tables, that he may run that readeth it. For the vision is yet for an appointed time, but at the end it shall speak, and not lie: though it tarry, wait for it; because it will surely come, it will not tarry." You can count on God, if He said it, it shall surely come to pass. The fact that you have not received the answer does not imply that God has not heard your prayer. The songwriter, Patrick Love wrote these profound words:

> "Write the vision, make it plain
> That they may run, and not faint
> Though the vision, is only for a while
> It shall speak, and not lie
> For if the Lord said it, you can count on it
> He will do, just what He said
> It is so, Yes it is so, He will do, just what He said."

The following confessions will infuse your spirit with renewed hope, strength and will lift you up:

• He promised, I will be with you always even unto the ends of the earth.

• I am believing in Him, I am trusting in Him, I am hoping in Him, He is working on my behalf.

- I am relying on Him and holding onto His promises, my God will not fail me.

- I know my redeemer liveth.

- I know He has not brought me this far to abandon me in confusion, misery and disappointment.

- I know my God will make a way for me.

- I know God will never put me to shame.

- I know that I am the head and not the tail.

- I know He will never leave me nor will He forsake me.

- I know that many are the afflictions of the righteous, but I know my God will deliver me from all, not some of them.

- I know a thousand will fall at my side and ten thousand on my right hand, it shall not come near me.

- I will call upon Him and He shall answer; He will be with me in my trouble and will deliver me.

- I know when I walk through the valley of the shadow of death, I shall fear no evil for thou art with me.

- When I pass through the waters, He will be with

me. When I walk through the rivers it will not overflow me. When I walk through the fires, I will not be burned, since I am precious in His sight.

- Even the Lord will slay me, yet will I still trust in Him, if I live, I live for Him; and if I die, I die for Him.

- I am more than a conqueror through Him that loved me.

- I know that all things are working for my good because He is the rewarder of those who diligently seek Him.

- Nothing will be able to separate me from the love of God.

- I know that no weapon that is formed against me shall prosper.

- He that is in me is greater than the things that are coming against me.

- I know that God is for me and He is not against me.

- I will live to see the goodness of the Lord in the land of the living.

- I know He's Almightly, All knowing, All sufficient and the God of all flesh and nothing is too hard for Him to do for me.

- I know the joy of the Lord is my strength.

- I know that Christ in me is the hope of glory

- I know I am weeping today, but my joy will come in the morning.

In closing, this is a promise from the Lord for us to meditate on, Isaiah 49:15 says, "Can a woman forget her sucking child, that she should not have compassion on the son of her womb? yea, they may forget, yet will I not forget thee." No one can tell or explain to you the reason your prayer is being delayed, but God knows why, wait for Him. At this point all that you can do is to take God at His Word concerning His promises. In other words, judge him to be faithful and encourage yourself in the Lord, your God. In I Samuel 30:3-4,6,18-19, it is said of King David:

"So David and his men came to the city, and, behold, *it was* burned with fire; and their wives, and their sons, and their daughters, were taken captives. Then David and the people that *were* with him lifted up their voice and wept, until they had no more power to weep. And David was greatly distressed; for the people spake of stoning him, because the soul of all the people was grieved, every man for his sons and for his daughters: but David encouraged himself in the Lord his God.... And David recovered all that the Amalekites had carried away: and David rescued his two wives. And there was nothing lacking to them, neither small nor great, neither sons nor daughters, neither spoil, nor any *thing* that they had taken to them: David recovered all."

King David and his men were distressed; they wept till

their strength had weaned. They did not have energy to weep anymore, but David encouraged himself in the Lord. Encourage yourself with these words and you will recover all.

Works Cited

Bounds, E. M. (1996). The Weapon of Prayer. New Kensington, PA: Whitaker House, pp 25.

Cho, David Yonggi. (1989). The Holy Spirit, My Senior Partner. Lake Mary, FL: Charisma House, pp 28-29.

Coleman, Robert E. (2000). The Master Plan Of Evangelism. Grand Rapids, MI: Baker Book House, pp 51, 52.

Eastman, Dick. (1999). The Hour That Changes the World. Grand Rapids, MI: Baker Book House, pp 116.

Evans Jr., James H. (1992). We Have Been Believers. Minneapolis, MN: Fortress Press, pp 47.

Finch, Raymond. (2002). The Power of Prayer. Boca Raton, FL: American Media Mini Mags, Inc., pp 38, 41.

Foxe, John. (1998). Foxe's Christian Martyrs of the World. Uhrichsville, OH: Barbour Publishing, Inc., pp 9.

Franklin, Jentezen. (2008). Fasting. Lake Mary, FL: Charisma House, pp 111.

George, Elizabeth. (1997/2006). A Woman After God's Own Heart. Eugene, Oregon: Harrison House Publishing, pp 31.

Gibbs, Eddie. (2000). Church Next. Downers Grove, IL: Inter Varsity Press, pp 15-16.

Graham, Franklin. (2006, May 29). Questions for Franklin Graham. Time Magazine, 167, pp 8.

Hill, George and Hazel. (2006). Fasting for Breakthrough and Revival. City, ST: Victory International Publishing, pp 12.

Hinn, Benny. (2005). Prayer That Gets Results. Dallas, TX: Clarion Call Marketing, pp 134, 151.

Hsu, Tom. (2007). Integrated Science: An Investigative Approach. Second Edition. Nashua, NH: CPO Science, pp 54-55.

Hunter, Charles and Frances. (2001). Handbook for Healing. Kingwood, TX: Whitaker House, pp 223.

Jones, Clifton. (2002). The Prayer Clinic Manual. Cincinnati, OH: Bethesda Ministries, Inc. pp 23.

Migliore, Daniel L. (2002). Faith Seeking Understanding. Grand Rapids, MI: Eerdmans Publishing Company, pp 120.

Munroe, Myles (2002). Understanding the Purpose and Power of Prayer. New Kensington, PA: Whitaker House, pp 222-223, 228.

Prince, Derek. (1970). Restoration Through Fasting. Ashanti, Ghana: Permission by Union of Christian Fellowship.

Robinson, Haddon W. (2002). Biblical Preaching. Grand Rapids, MI: Baker Academic, pp 169

Smith, Michael W., & King, W. (2002). There She Stands. *Worship Again* [CD]. Franklin, TN: MMII Reunion Records, Inc.

Tertullian, Apologeticum. (Apology) 50,13.

Wallis, Arthur. (1999). God's Chosen Fast. Fort Washington, PA: Christian Literature Crusade, pp 109, 115.

Warren, Rick. (2002). The Purpose Driven Life. Grand Rapids, MI: Zondervan, pp 133.

Webster's New World College Dictionary. Fourth Edition. (1999). New York, NY: Macmillan USA, 99 1130.

William Tyndale College: Academic Catalog 2001-2002. Farmington Hills, MI, pp 8.

Williams, Dave R. (2004). The Miracle Results of Fasting. Tulsa, OK: Harrison House Publishers, pp 15-16, 17, 23-24.

On-Line Articles:

A Butterfly Story. (n.d.). Retrieved August 21, 2008, from http://awesomebutterflies.com/a_butterfly_story.htm

The Four Boyfriends. (n.d.). Retrieved October 18, 2007, from http://www.beyondhorizoncoaching.com

The Heavens Gate. (n.d.). Retrieved July 11, 2001, from http://www.stelling.nl/simpos/ heavgate.htm

The Lords of Chaos. (n.d.). Retrieved March 3, 2002, from http://www.jim-greenhill.com/page322450.htm

Ganther, I. (n.d.). The People's Temple. Retrieved July 11, 2001, from http://www.owlnet.rice.edu/~reli291/Jonestown/ Jonestown.html

Keathy, H. (n.d.). The Uniqueness of Jesus Christ. Retrieved December 24, 2002, from http://bible.org/ docs/ pastor/seasonal/xmas/unique.htm

Oatman, Jr., Johnson. (1895). No Not One. Favorite Hymns of the Firemen by The Fireman. Retrieved March 21, 2008, from http://www.acadisc.com/firemenfav.htm

NOTES: